Tales from the Browns Sideline

Tony Grossi

Sports Publishing L.L.C.
www.sportspublishingllc.com

Director of production: Susan M. Moyer
Developmental editor: Kipp Wilfong
Project manager: Alicia D. Wentworth
Copy editor: Cynthia L. McNew
Photo editor: Erin Linden-Levy
Dust jacket design: Heidi Norsen
Imaging: Dustin Hubbart
Acquisitions editor: Mike Pearson

ISBN: 1-58261-713-9

Printed in the United States of America.

Sports Publishing L.L.C.
www.sportspublishingllc.com

*To my wife and best friend, Carolyn, my Kitch,
whose faith in me fueled the energy to proceed
with this project.*

CONTENTS

ACKNOWLEDGMENTS

Mike Pearson, vice president of acquisitions at Sports Publishing L.L.C., contacted me about doing this book in December of 2002. My first thought was no. Lucky for me, he persisted. If not, I would have regretted it the rest of my life.

Russell Schneider was there early to provide encouragement and support. The very sight of his books in my office was inspiration. So were the works of many other fine authors and colleagues such as Bob Dolgan, Terry Pluto, Paul Tepley, John Steadman, Jon Morgan and John Keim.

This book would not have been written without the help and guidance of Dino Lucarelli, Browns manager of alumni relations extraordinaire. Dino is the unofficial walking, talking Browns history book. His contributions of time always go beyond the call of duty.

Sam Rutigliano was my first interview. After talking with him for two hours, I was excited about going forward. Bill Belichick gave me more than one hour of his time between winning Super Bowls. Ernie Accorsi's storytelling and vast recollection of events are priceless. Peter Hadhazy filled in a lot of missing pieces.

I am thankful to all of them, plus all the players and coaches who shared their stories with me. Some of them were 50 years removed from the playing days, and listening to them opened my eyes to things I could not see before.

INTRODUCTION

Remember the Cleveland Bulldogs? I didn't think so. A team by that name competed in the National Football League in the 1924, 1925 and 1927 seasons. Partly with that historical link in mind, some people liked Bulldogs as the name for Cleveland's expansion franchise in 1999.

Those fans were hurt and hardened by the series of events that allowed Art Modell to move the Cleveland Browns to Baltimore in 1996. They didn't want the replacement team to carry the same name as the glorious franchise that was birthed and nurtured by Paul Brown. They wanted the new team to start with a wholly new identity and no history.

Fortunately it didn't happen that way.

The NFL and the city of Cleveland insisted that Modell leave the Browns' name, colors and history behind in the global settlement that freed him to go to Baltimore to dodge personal bankruptcy.

It was a wise decision. Continuing the Browns' name and history after a three-year hiatus kept Lou Groza and Dante Lavelli in the Cleveland record books. It connected Otto Graham to Tim Couch, Jim Brown to Ben Gay, and all the great Browns players—and great characters—to those who would follow in 1999 and beyond so that when coach Chris Palmer gathered the first new Browns players in the summer of 1999, he was able to show them a grainy, black and white video telling the story of the franchise so rich in tradition that preceded them.

And a whole generation of fans would learn for the first time the real characters who first wore the simple white and brown uniforms with the plain orange helmets.

This work seeks to strengthen the connection between the old Browns and the new Browns. The three-year period in which football was not played in Cleveland should never be forgotten. But it may be reduced, over time, to nothing more than a hiccup in the history of one of the NFL's most storied and colorful franchises.

The subjects profiled here were selected by me, as was the order of tales listed. Some were chosen for their obvious contributions to the evolution of the franchise. Others were selected because of the inspiration of their stories. Hanford Dixon and Frank Minnifield are the only ones who share the same profile. It was impossible to separate them.

The book is heavy on profiles from the mid-1980s. That was the beginning of my era as Browns beat writer for *The Plain Dealer*. It is also an era that hasn't been recorded in book form prior to now.

This is by no means a comprehensive list. Dozens of instrumental players and deserving characters were omitted— even some Hall of Famers—and for that, I apologize. There certainly are enough stories left untold to fill up a second edition of Browns tales.

CHAPTER 1

The 1940s and 1950s

PAUL BROWN

The history of the Cleveland Browns begins with the arrival of Paul Brown as founding coach in 1945, 18 months before they played their first game. Already considered a coaching legend in Ohio when he accepted a $25,000 salary from owner Arthur McBride at the age of 36, Brown dominated the franchise for the next 17 years.

Brown named the new team after himself and created it in his image. His stated goal was to make the Browns the New York Yankees and the Joe Louis of pro football. He styled the team's uniforms and chose the colors of white, orange and brown. When other teams adopted logos in the 1950s and affixed them to their helmets, Brown obstinately left his helmets plain, a distinction only the Browns hold today.

Brown pioneered numerous innovations that are now commonplace in pro football, such as the use of playbooks, game film study, and giving his players mental aptitude tests. He

Paul Brown (Photo by Paul Tepley)

was the first to appoint full-time assistant coaches at each position and the first coach in the All-America Football Conference to sign African-American players.

"Before Paul Brown came along, they just rolled the ball out on the field for practice," Hall of Fame coach Sid Gillman once said.

"He's the guy that changed football, not Red Grange or George Halas," said receiver Dante Lavelli.

The Browns dominated the AAFC, winning each of the four championships and compiling a record of 52-4-3. They caused the league to disband from lack of interest. The Browns joined the established National Football League in 1950 with two other AAFC teams.

For their first game in 1950, the NFL scheduled the Browns against the Philadelphia Eagles, who had won the previous two league championships. The Browns whipped them, 35-10.

"That was a moment of triumph for him," recalled Mike Brown, Paul's son. "I think he took pleasure in that game almost beyond what he took from any other."

The Browns went on to win the NFL championship in their first season. They also won in 1954 and '55. They played in the championship game but lost in 1951, '52, '53 and '57.

"He ran the show. He was the greatest ever," said quarterback Otto Graham.

Brown ruled his team like a dictator and demanded that his players follow strict rules. Most loathed his tyrannical ways—until their careers were over.

"Everyone complained when they played for him, but those that went into coaching all tried to be like him when they retired," said Jackie Groza, wife of Lou.

"If you did your job, he never said a thing," Lavelli said. "He never swore at you. If you did something wrong, he'd bore right through you with those beady eyes and tell you off. After he left the practice field, he'd never hold a grudge against you."

Mike Brown said: "Even when my dad's teams were winning year after year, those guys were almost always in a state of semi-rebellion because he was a taskmaster and he had a sharp tongue.

"Yet by the fact he held them to such a demanding standard, he got the best out of them. I think at a certain point, they began to realize that, not always even when they were playing."

The Browns did not have a losing season until 1956, the year Graham retired for the second and last time. By the 1960s, players were privately saying the game was passing Brown by and he was too stubborn to adapt.

The end for Brown began when Art Modell, a 35-year-old advertising executive from Brooklyn, New York, bought the

Browns in 1961. Modell gave Brown an eight-year contract, but their clashing egos made it apparent that they could not coexist.

After two years together, which Brown called "the darkest period in my life," Modell called Brown into his office and fired him.

"He was shaken, which was not like him," Mike Brown said more than 40 years later. "His statement was that Modell had taken his team away from him. Other than family tragedies, I think that was the biggest blow of his life."

Brown returned to Ohio after a five-year exile and founded his second franchise, the Cincinnati Bengals. He coached them to the playoffs in their third year and into the Super Bowl in their 14th.

He was inducted into the Pro Football Hall of Fame in 1967.

Former NFL commissioner Pete Rozelle once was asked to name the most important owner during his 30-year tenure. He said George Halas and Art Rooney had to be on board for anything to get done. Rozelle said Brown, though, had the biggest impact.

"He made the game better for the players and the fans both," Rozelle said.

OTTO GRAHAM

Otto Graham suffered from Alzheimer's disease in the final years of his life, but it did not curb his flair for storytelling.

"I may have Alzheimer's, but I'm still full of BS, you know," Graham said cheerfully from his home in Sarasota, Florida, in the spring of 2003.

Graham died from a heart aneuryism seven months later.

He was the first player signed by Paul Brown in 1946 when the coach assembled the Browns after World War II. In the vernacular of football, no player in the next 50 years would rival Graham as a field general.

He led the Browns to 10 consecutive league championship games—four in the All-America Football Conference, winning them all, and six in the NFL, winning three.

But don't credit Graham for being "in charge" of the Browns' dynasty.

"'In charge' are the wrong words," he insisted. "Paul Brown was in charge. He ran the show."

The quarterback and coach sparred occasionally over Brown's insistence on calling every play on the field. Their mutual respect for each other kept the relationship healthy for a 10-year run of excellence that may never be seen again in the NFL.

"He'd bring in the plays with messenger guards," Graham said. "Sometimes I ignored it and called something else. But I guarantee you one thing—if I didn't do what he sent in, I better damn well make some yards, or I'd be in trouble."

The defining moment of their relationship occurred in the NFL championship game of 1950. The Browns were cast as upstarts in their first year in the haughty, established league. They advanced to play for the league title against the Los Angeles Rams—the very franchise that left Cleveland in 1946 rather than compete with the popular Brown's new team.

The Browns were behind, 28-27, and driving with the ball late in the game. Graham ran on a quarterback draw and was hit from the blind side. He fumbled and the Rams recovered with three minutes to go.

Otto Graham (Photo courtesy of Cleveland Press Collection, CSU)

On his way to the sideline, Graham thought Brown surely would chew him out for blowing the game. To his surprise, the stern coach patted him on the shoulder and said, "Don't worry, Otts. We'll get the ball back for you and win this thing yet."

"There aren't enough words in the dictionary to adequately describe how he bolstered my confidence and lifted my spirits," Graham recalled.

Brown was right. The Browns got the ball back, and Graham took the team down with a run and three completions. Lou Groza kicked the winning field goal with 28 seconds left for what is considered one of the greatest upsets in NFL history.

Dante Lavelli, who caught more of Graham's passes than any receiver, said, "You know what his main forte was? Being cool under pressure."

In his 1979 autobiography, *PB—The Paul Brown Story*, Brown wrote, "As far as I'm concerned, Otto Graham was the greatest player in the game's history."

Graham modestly refutes the assertion.

"It's nice to hear," he said. "But you might put a few other guys in there. You can't say who was the best ever. Was I a good player? Yes. I had good coordination. I could throw the ball accurately. I could run well."

When the Pro Football Hall of Fame calculated a formula to compare quarterbacks of different eras, Graham's ranking stood as No. 1 through the 1980s until Joe Montana's statistics eclipsed him. The formula did not incorporate championships won.

Graham was inducted in the third class of the Hall of Fame in 1965. Until his death, he was an occasional visitor to Canton and Cleveland. The pool of fans who actually saw him play shrinks every year, but his stature in the history of the game is passed on through generations.

"If you're winning most every game and the press writes it up as a great team and all that stuff, you have to enjoy that," he said of his prime years. "If you don't enjoy that, you're in the wrong profession. But Paul Brown didn't let us get too worked up over it because he didn't want any prima donnas on the team."

Graham's one regret is that he didn't return to music after retiring.

His mother and father were accomplished musicians. In his high school and college years, Graham played the French horn in a brass sextet that won competitions. He also played the oboe, cornet, violin and piano.

"Piano, that's the one I should have kept up," he said. "I can't play football right now, but I could still be playing piano today. I'd still be the life of the party."

LOU GROZA

The lasting image of Lou Groza is of a very large man with a belly protruding over his belt, fully extending his right leg, swinging his black leather, high-top kicking shoe with a square toe through a ball and pummelling it between the goal posts.

The Smithsonian Institution anointed Groza as the quintessential football place-kicker by keeping a pair of his size 12 black high-tops on display. College football gives an award in his name to the season's best kicker.

But while he spent the last eight seasons of his 21-year career as the NFL's first kicking specialist, fortifying his enduring nickname "the Toe," Groza first and foremost was a left offensive tackle.

"He was proud of the fact he went in the Pro Football Hall of Fame as a tackle," said his widow, Jackie. "All of the Hall of Famers have a ring that says the position they played. His says tackle."

It could have said winner. In 21 seasons with the Browns, Groza played in 13 league championship games in the All-America Football Conference and NFL. The Browns won eight of them.

He became Paul Brown's starting left tackle in 1948 and held the position through the 1959 season, while doubling as the kicker. He made the all-NFL team six times as a tackle and was named NFL player of the year in 1954.

A back injury caused him to sit out the 1960 season and retire. After Art Modell purchased the Browns in 1961, he enticed Groza out of retirement to return as a full-time kicker. Groza was the last of the original 1946 Browns to retire.

Groza still holds club and NFL kicking records. His 16-yard field goal with 28 seconds left gave the Browns a 30-28 win over the Los Angeles Rams in the 1950 NFL championship in their first year in the established league.

"Everyone remembers that as his highlight," said Jackie. "That was the year we were married. But the one in high school was important to him, too."

Groza was a three-sport star in high school in Martins Ferry, an Ohio River town near Wheeling, West Virginia. Jackie said Lou never forgot the time he helped his high school basketball team to the state championship with two free throws in a semifinal game.

"He was fouled on the last play of the game. The game was tied. He was the worst foul shooter on the team. He shot the

Lou Groza (Photo by Paul Tepley)

first one in to win the game and just threw the other one in, too. It was so exciting for him," she said.

Groza was a favorite of Paul Brown. The unsentimental coach called Groza "my Louie."

"He loved Paul," said Jackie. "Paul was strict and a great disciplinarian. He and Paul were friends.

"We always used to laugh at the fact we were all scared to death of Paul Brown. One time, we were going to meet for a picnic at the park in Brecksville. We were going to meet Don Colo and his wife and we got lost in the park. And they were to have a [team] meeting at night, and Lou was absolutely frantic because he just knew they were going to be in trouble. Thankfully, we found our way and dropped him off in time for the meeting."

After retirement in 1968, Groza became a fixture in the Cleveland community and at Browns alumni functions. Despite a back surgery, two hip surgeries and a late bout with Parkinson's disease, Groza reveled in the legendary status his playing career earned him.

One of his greatest thrills, Jackie said, was having a street named in his honor in Berea, where they lived since getting married in 1950. The address of Browns headquarters, in fact, is 76 Lou Groza Blvd. The number was Groza's jersey number. He died at the age of 76 after a heart attack in 2000.

One of Groza's last public appearances came at the Pro Football Hall of Fame Game in Canton when the Browns played their first exhibition game after being reborn as an expansion team in 1999.

Groza was introduced on the national television broadcast of the game as "Hall of Fame kicker Lou Groza."

Slightly irritated, Groza looked at the interviewer and corrected, "I was a left tackle."

DANTE LAVELLI

D ante Lavelli's nickname of "Gluefingers" became a euphemism for all sure-handed receivers who would follow. But he was the first to earn it.

An original member of the Browns, Lavelli was an integral part of the offensive machine built by Paul Brown that played in 10 consecutive league championship games and won seven.

He played in only three games at Ohio State before leaving to fight in World War II. He served 35 months in the 28th Army Infantry and fought in the Battle of Bulge.

When he returned to join Brown's new team in the All-America Football Conference in 1946, Lavelli was a virtual unknown.

"Nobody knew me," he said. "We had an intrasquad game at Bowling Green. Cliff Lewis was the quarterback because Otto Graham was at the college All-Star game.

"So I'm out there catching the ball one-handed, two-handed, jumping in the air. Bob Neal was the radio play-by-play announcer. One day he goes into the lunch room and says to Paul Brown, 'Who's that guy catching everything out there, like he's got gluefingers?'"

Before he retired in 1956, Lavelli would catch 386 passes—though the NFL does not acknowledge the 142 receptions in the four championship years the Browns dominated the AAFC.

The cold shoulder given by the NFL to the Browns' early years in the rival league was always a sore point for the outspoken Lavelli.

He believes the Browns' 29-game unbeaten streak in the AAFC—which includes a 15-0 season and league championship in 1948—should be recognized by the NFL.

Dante Lavelli (Photo courtesy of Cleveland Press Collection, CSU)

"It burns me up," Lavelli said. "If it was the New York Yankees that had the record, they sure would publicize it."

The perfect '48 season included a whirlwind week in which the Browns won three games on the road in eight days. They beat the Yankees in New York, the Dons in Los Angeles and the 49ers in San Francisco during Thanksgiving week.

"We didn't practice between them; didn't need to," Lavelli said. "They weren't cupcakes, either."

Lavelli earned Brown's respect as a clutch player by having consistently strong performances in the team's biggest games. He had 24 catches in the Browns' six NFL title games. But he cherishes most the winning touchdown he caught in the first AAFC title game against the Yankees in 1946.

"It started the Browns on their way," he said. "It didn't mean so much then, but as time goes on, it builds."

Lavelli chuckles recalling another of his favorite stories—when he beat the Philadelphia Eagles in a 1954 game by swinging around the goalpost and losing his defender in the end zone.

"The field was icy," he said. "I was supposed to go across the middle, but I hooked the post on the last play of the game and went to the right and was wide open. Everybody went the other way because they couldn't stop. I was the last guy to do that because they moved the goalposts back to the end line [in 1966]."

Brown once called Lavelli "the toughest player I ever coached."

Lavelli was elected to the Pro Football Hall of Fame in 1975. The native of Hudson, Ohio, never left Cleveland after his playing days.

Impeccably dressed and dapper, the white-haired Lavelli was a fixture at his furniture and appliance store in Rocky River for more than 40 years.

BILL WILLIS

More than 50 years after he helped integrate blacks into professional football, Bill Willis speaks modestly, almost apologetically, about his place in American history.

"A lot of times when you are directly involved in something, you don't grasp the situation as to what it really is," he said. "To me at that time, it was simply a desire to play football and make the very best of the situation presented to me."

Willis was the first black player signed by Paul Brown when he formed his first team in the All-America Football Conference in 1946. About a week later, Brown added fullback Marion Motley, ostensibly to be Willis's roommate and companion.

Earlier that year, the Los Angeles Rams of the NFL reopened the door to African-Americans when they signed halfback Kenny Washington and lineman Woody Strode. They were the NFL's first black players since 1933.

But they were ordinary players who dropped out of the league in three years. Willis and Motley not only endured, they starred for a team rapidly gaining a national profile. They would become the flag bearers for the full integration of the sport.

"You know, so much has happened since then," Willis said. "You look back at the game today and you can see a lot of black ballplayers. You also see how well they intermingle and get along.

"So you look at that and you think, 'Well, I did have a part of that in the beginning.' One of the fortunate things for me, I believe, is that I played in the Big Ten [for Ohio State] and in so doing I played against or with an awful lot of the ballplayers who played pro ball. I knew a lot of them and was familiar with them, so it became easy to laugh and talk and feel comfortable."

From left: Gene Hickerson, Otto Graham, Gary Collins, Lou Groza, Bill Willis (Photo by Paul Tepley)

Willis recalls Brown holding him and Motley out of a trip to Miami because the city outlawed whites and blacks playing together on the same field in 1946.

"A lot of stuff was happening that I was totally unaware of," Willis said. "Paul talked to me and to Motley, separately, and said he would not take us to Miami and subject us to any unpleasant things. He said we can beat them anyway, and this wouldn't happen again because they won't be in the league next year."

The Browns beat Miami, 34-0, without Willis and Motley. As Brown predicted, Miami was out of the league in 1947.

Willis was a middle guard, stationed over center in the five-man defensive front that was in vogue at the time. Despite being only 6'2" and 199 pounds, he became known as Big Bill Willis.

His quickness became legendary after his first scrimmage with the Browns, when he repeatedly beat center Mike (Mo) Scarry and frustrated quarterback Otto Graham.

"The coaches told me I was doing a lot of things I wasn't supposed to as middle guard, like making tackles in the backfield," Willis said. "Paul would have me pull out sometimes to the left and right, to bat down those little passes, like a linebacker.

"Paul often said I was the forerunner to middle linebacker. Actually, the middle guard was not supposed to go in and make the tackle. But because of the fact I played tackle at Ohio State, I couldn't help but go in. I had the mentality to be right in the quarterback's face. At the same time, I knew that my responsibilities were to go from side to side.

"I was fairly fast for a middle guard. At Ohio State and with the Browns, I used to run the sprints with the backs. I think a lot of times Paul would do that just to embarrass some of the backs."

Willis's reputation was enhanced in a goal line stand that secured a Browns 8-3 playoff victory over the New York Giants in their first NFL season in 1950.

Willis ran down Gene (Choo Choo) Roberts at the four after a 32-yard gain. The Giants were forced to kick a field goal after Willis threw another ball carrier for a five-yard loss. Willis also had a safety in the game. The next week, they beat the Los Angeles Rams, 30-28, for the NFL championship.

"A lot of things happened that I do not recall," Willis said, at a loss to describe the epochal defensive series.

Willis was inducted in the Pro Football Hall of Fame in 1977. By then 10 other blacks had been enshrined. They could thank Willis for blazing the trail to football immortality.

MARION MOTLEY

Sometimes Paul Brown stumbled upon greatness through sheer accident. Such was the case with Marion Motley, the greatest fullback the NFL has ever seen.

Brown coached against Motley's team in high school, and then coached him at Great Lakes Naval Training Station during World War II. But when Motley asked for a tryout with the Browns in 1946, Brown responded that he had enough fullbacks.

Brown changed his mind after breaking the color barrier in the All-America Football Conference and signing middle guard Bill Willis. It was commonly believed that Brown then signed Motley as a roommate and companion for Willis.

According to Emerson Cole, who became Motley's closest friend upon joining the Browns in 1950, Brown had to be talked into bringing Motley aboard.

"After Paul Brown sent Marion back to Canton, the Canton business people had a meeting with Paul Brown and somehow changed his mind, which is very difficult," Cole said.

Motley led the AAFC in rushing each of the four years the Browns dominated, and then led the NFL in 1950. He became known as "Otto Graham's bodyguard" because his blocking kept rushers off the quarterback's back. Motley was 6'1" and 232 pounds.

"He elongated the life of Otto Graham," Cole said.

Even the "Motley trap," one of the early staples of Brown's play calling, happened by accident.

"The Motley trap came because of a mistake," said Dante Lavelli. "One of the backs was supposed to get the ball. Otto turned around, but only Marion was back there, to block. So

Marion Motley (Photo courtesy of Cleveland Press Collection, CSU)

Otto gave the ball to Marion and he goes up the middle and there's nobody there. It became the Motley trap."

Graham remembered it slightly differently.

"I went back to pass and I thought I was going to get murdered because our line broke down," he said. "So I just handed the ball to Marion Motley. He was back there to block. And he took off and made some good yardage. They all thought I had the ball. It wasn't planned, but it was so successful that Paul Brown put it in the playbook the very next game."

By the time the Browns were absorbed into the NFL in 1950, Motley was 30 and had two bad knees. He had taken a pounding as an inside runner and a blocker, and he also was used as a linebacker in goal line and short-yardage situations.

"The bad part of it was Mot was two or three years older than the rest of us and he didn't get to play [in the NFL] in his prime," Lavelli said. "He gained a little weight at the end and he had real bad feet. His shoes never fit him right. He'd always come in the huddle and say, 'Don't step on my feet.'"

Motley had enough gas to lead the NFL in rushing with 810 yards on 140 carries in 1950. In one game against Pittsburgh, he amassed 188 yards on 11 carries. That 17.09-yard average remains an NFL record for one game.

"The trap was a fantastic play, but I was seldom sent outside," Motley once said. "There's no telling how much yardage I might have made if I ran as much as some backs do now."

Motley averaged 6.2 yards a rush in four years in the AAFC and 5.0 yards in primarily four years in the NFL. Combining both leagues, his career average was 5.7 yards. That figure dwarfs the official NFL record for a running back of 5.22 by Jim Brown.

Being one of the NFL's first black players, Motley endured abuse on and off the field.

"He could handle it," Cole said. "They [opposing white players] stomped on his hands, kicked him in the head. That stuff went on constantly.

"He was a gentleman and a very religious guy. He stayed at my house a lot and we were roommates on the road. I never saw him go to bed without getting on his knees and never saw him take a bite of food without blessing it.

"Motley was one of a kind. He didn't have a lot of education, but what he didn't have in education he made up in mother wit. He made wise decisions that helped to perpetuate the integration of football and baseball."

In 1968, Motley became the second African-American inducted into the Pro Football Hall of Fame. He died in 1999 of prostate cancer.

At Motley's funeral, Joe Perry, a running back with San Francisco also in the Hall of Fame, said, "I had to come. Marion's my man. He was the greatest all-around football player there ever was."

DUB JONES

The most sensational performance in Browns' history belongs to William Jones.

Jones—nicknamed Dub by Louisiana relatives because of his first initial "Double U"—scored six touchdowns in a 42-21 victory over the Chicago Bears in a game in Cleveland Municipal Stadium on November 25, 1951.

Jones scored touchdowns on runs of two, 12, 27 and 42 yards, and on catches of 34 and 43 yards. He scored the last five times he touched the ball.

The outburst equaled the league record of six touchdowns set by Ernie Nevers of the Chicago Cardinals in 1929. Bears running back Gale Sayers matched it in 1965.

Jones, the starting halfback, ran nine times for 116 yards and caught three passes for 80 yards. His record day wasn't the only thing unusual about the game.

The Browns were penalized 21 times for 209 yards, and the Bears had 16 penalties for 165 yards. The totals remain NFL records.

"It's a shame a performance like Dub's had to come in a game like this," Paul Brown said after the game.

Jones, a 6'4", 205-pound halfback and flanker, played from 1948 through 1955. Brown teamed up Jones with Dante Lavelli and Mac Speedie in a formidable three-receiver offense that was ahead of its time. Defenses could not cope with the triple threat because no teams had anything comparable to it.

After retirement, Jones served as Blanton Collier's offensive backfield coach from 1963 to '68. His son, Bert, was a first-round draft choice of the Baltimore Colts in 1973 and played 10 years in the NFL.

EMERSON COLE

P ro football was closed to African-American players from 1933 to 1946. Technically, the Browns were the second pro football team to reopen the sport to blacks. The NFL Los Angeles Rams signed two black players in 1946 before Paul Brown signed Bill Willis and Marion Motley.

But Brown was the first coach to sign blacks in the newly formed All-America Football Conference.

"When they had a meeting to start the All-America league, he voted with them unanimously not to use any blacks, and then he went and signed Bill Willis," said Emerson Cole.

Cole joined the Browns in 1950 as the first black player drafted by Brown. He was the fifth black player on the team, following Willis, Motley, Horace Gillom and Len Ford, who originally joined the Los Angeles Dons of the AAFC in 1948.

Cole was drafted to replace Motley as Browns fullback. He played three years and couldn't dislodge Motley from the line-up.

"When I came in, I was 22 and Motley was 30," Cole said. "Motley was still playing in '51. I kept asking him, 'Man, why don't you rest those old knees of yours?' He said, 'Oh, no. If I sit down, I'll never get back up.'"

Motley took Cole under his wing, and the two men struck a friendship that lasted until Motley died in 1999.

Cole left Toledo with a bachelor's degree in education. His family had sent him to predominantly white schools. He didn't realize what he didn't know until he got to the NFL in 1950.

"When I got to Cleveland, it was a whole new world," he said, referring to the racial tensions at the time. "I was a pretty good pugilist in my time. I was going to punch a couple cats out. Motley advised against it. He pulled me away a couple times.

"1950 was the worst of all, really. I didn't know about staying in separate hotels and eating in separate restaurants. That was quite an awakening for me."

Cole credits Brown for the integration of football, but he said the coach merely recognized the athletic prowess of black players.

"The trouble I had with him was he didn't think blacks had much intellect," Cole said. "He certainly admired their physical ability, but he never gave them much credit for thinking and intelligence.

"He and I never got along. It was probably because I never went to any black schools in my life and when I talked to someone, I'd look at him square in the eyes. That seemed to be forbidden and I didn't know it. My dad taught me that when you talk to a person, look him in the eye. I didn't know that wasn't right."

Cole's experiences in the NFL shaped the rest of his life.

"[Redskins owner] George Preston Marshall said he wanted Paul Brown to play without his blacks," Cole recalled. "He asked if he could and Paul Brown said yeah he could, but he couldn't win. We beat them 45-0.

"One of Detroit's owners, Walter Briggs, he said he would rather we didn't play on his field because the acid would come through our shoes and kill his grass. Here's a businessman who's dumb enough to think that acid would go from a black man's foot and into the grass."

Cole retired at the age of 25. The majority of his life then was spent working with the U.S. Civil Rights Commission.

"After the treatment I saw in football, I had no desire to teach kids," he said. "I wanted to change factories, and systems. I wanted to teach on a bigger scale. I wanted to help the affected classes and change the attitude of companies. I spent my entire life in that endeavor."

CHUCK NOLL

The modern rivalry between the Browns and the Pittsburgh Steelers really begins with Chuck Noll.

The Browns and Steelers played twice a season starting in 1950, but until Noll was hired as Steelers coach and transformed them into winners, this rivalry was one-sided.

The Browns won 28 of 38 meetings and never lost twice in a year to the Steelers from 1950 through 1968. After Noll became Steelers coach in 1969, Pittsburgh won 22 of the next 34 meetings, including 16 times in a row in Three Rivers Stadium.

Built by cunning drafting, Noll's teams won four Super Bowls in a six-year span in the 1970s. His teams sent nine players to the Hall of Fame. Noll was inducted in 1993.

Pittsburgh's greatest coach was a product of Cleveland's Benedictine High School, the University of Dayton and Paul Brown.

Noll aspired to coaching, rather than playing, until Brown made him a 20th-round draft choice in 1953. By signing his Browns contract, Noll turned down an offer to be Benedictine's football coach before the legendary Augie Bossu.

Noll would later start for the Browns at outside linebacker for three seasons, but is best remembered for being one of Brown's original "messenger" guards. He'd run in Brown's play calls on every other play.

"It was a learning experience for me," Noll said 50 years later. "In fact, I think it helped me when I got into coaching. It taught me how to put a game plan together."

Like most of his teammates, however, Noll didn't like Brown's stiff control of his offense. As Pittsburgh's head coach, Noll never called his quarterback's plays.

"That was one of the learning experiences," he said. "I thought when I'd come in with a play [as a messenger guard], the quarterbacks—Otto [Graham], especially—really wanted that on his shoulders. I thought that the quarterback needed to do that to get the respect of the rest of the players. That's one of the reasons we didn't do it at Pittsburgh.

"We spent a lot of time in meetings preparing our quarterbacks to call them, so that we were on the same page, thinking the same way. What we tried to do was talk to them about a series—what do you want to get done?—before they went in, as opposed to calling each individual play. I thought that was the way to go."

Although he played in four NFL championship games, winning two, Noll's short playing career proved to be just a training ground for his coaching career. He was nicknamed "the Pope" by a coach at Dayton.

"That started at Benedictine," Noll said, laughing. "It changed from Know-it-All Noll to the Pope, because I was 'infallible.'"

Noll retired at age 27 in 1960 to join Sid Gillman with the Los Angeles Chargers of the fledgling American Football League. He later joined Don Shula in Baltimore and was on the Colts' staff when they lost Super Bowl III to Joe Namath's Jets.

"When we lost, everybody was in the tank, including me," Noll said. "That's when I got a few interviews [for head coach]."

He chose Pittsburgh over Buffalo and the Boston Patriots because he liked the patience and vision expressed by Steelers executive Dan Rooney.

Noll never got sentimental about returning to Cleveland as coach of his hometown's chief rival.

"It wasn't like Paul Brown was still there," he said of the Browns after his mentor was fired. "It was a different team completely … a different organization."

GEORGE RATTERMAN

In 1952, Paul Brown began looking for a successor to Otto Graham at quarterback. The coach traded for George Ratterman, a native of Cincinnati and a four-sport letter winner at Notre Dame.

Instead of Graham's successor, what Brown acquired was one of the team's all-time pranksters and practical jokers.

Ratterman would impersonate coaches in anonymous phone calls to unsuspecting victims, insert himself on the kickoff coverage team during games, and terrify teammates by secretly placing garter snakes in their lockers. Nobody was exempt from Ratterman's pranks.

"He was a real character," Graham said. "One time I was on the sideline and he was playing quarterback. Paul Brown sent in a rookie guard with the play. Ratterman told the young player, 'I don't like that play; go back and get another one.'"

The guard, Gene Donaldson, dutifully turned and headed back to the sideline to get another play from Brown. Players in the huddle laughed uproariously.

Not even Ratterman, though, could stand to imperil the young guard's future on Brown's team. He yelled him back to the huddle.

"Everybody laughed about that one for years," Graham said. "I always said I'd loved to have stood next to Paul Brown when that player asked for another play. He would've killed somebody."

Ratterman finally got his shot to start after Graham retired in 1956. He started four games before breaking an ankle. He retired after the season.

HORACE GILLOM

Horace Gillom played as a tight end and middle linebacker for Paul Brown at Massillon Washington High School and joined the Browns in 1947, a year after their inception. He became the franchise's best punter of all time.

He still has the three longest punts in team history. His career average of 43.82 yards per punt has stood for 47 years as the franchise record. Gillom led the NFL in punting in 1951 and 1952.

"I never saw any equal in punting," said 1950s teammate Emerson Cole. "He would tell us in the huddle, 'Go all out, because this one's going to hit going toward the other goal line.'

"Other times he would say, 'Be under control, because this one's going to hit and come back.' He could control how the ball bounced."

Gillom was the third African-American player signed by Brown following Bill Willis and Marion Motley. He died in 1985. Since Gillom retired in 1956, there have been only three other black punters in the NFL.

KEN CARPENTER

There was no hoopla to the college draft when the Browns joined the established NFL in 1950.

Ken Carpenter, the club's first-ever draft choice, learned of his selection in a letter from Paul Brown.

"I didn't read the sports page too much, so I didn't even know what was going on. It was a pleasant surprise," Carpenter recalled.

Carpenter was a running back with Oregon State. He held his school record for all-purpose yardage. He didn't even consider playing pro football until a Browns coach mentioned the possibility at a banquet after a college All-Star game.

After the draft, Carpenter was visited in Corvallis, Oregon, by a Browns coach carrying a contract.

"I got $6,500 and a $500 bonus," Carpenter said. "It was a lot of money to me. But they wouldn't give me the bonus until the college baseball season was over."

After Carpenter played in the annual College All-Star Game in Chicago, he hitchhiked to his first Browns training camp at Bowling Green with John Sandusky, who was Brown's second-round choice.

"Back then, you were just another player," Carpenter said. "I remember when they drafted Don Klosterman [in 1952]. He was going to be the successor to Otto Graham. It wasn't two weeks into training camp before he was released. They drove him to a bus stop and gave him a ticket home [to California]."

Carpenter played with the Browns four years. He alternated at running back and played on special teams. He was voted to the Pro Bowl after the 1952 season.

LEO MURPHY

Nobody had more years of service with the Browns than Leo Murphy.

He was hired as Browns trainer by Paul Brown in 1950, their first year in the NFL. Murphy served numerous other unofficial roles until he retired in 1992.

In the early days, Murphy was a point man for some of Brown's equipment innovations.

One was the facemask on the helmet. Before an injury to Otto Graham in a 1953 game, no players wore facemasks. Murphy designed a single bar screwed to the helmet, which offered some protection.

"A lot of guys didn't want to wear them because they had trouble seeing," Murphy recalled. "I told them it wasn't an option, the Old Man [Brown] said that everybody has to wear them.

"We're playing one day in Washington. Abe Gibron was one guard and Chuck Noll was the other. Chuck didn't like them at all. He was complaining all the time. He said, 'I'm not gonna wear it.' I gave him a screwdriver and said, 'If you don't want to wear it, here, take it off.'

"In the game, one of the guards was supposed to pull, but they both pulled and ran into each other right behind the quarterback. Noll came running out of the game holding his mouth and saying, 'I need the facemask, I need the facemask.' His two front teeth were out and he was bleeding like a stuck pig.

"I told him, 'You don't need it any more, baby.'"

Murphy also was the brains behind the original tearaway jersey in the late 1950s.

"I came up with the idea," he said. "A lot of times, guys would grab the nylon jersey and bring down a player with a couple of fingers, just pulling on the jersey. I had Champion make some tearaway jerseys. They weren't the regular quality, but they looked the same.

"We were playing Philadelphia and we went through about eight jerseys between Bobby Mitchell and Jim Brown in the first half. Instead of tackling them, they'd just break away. We found out the bad thing was you had to take a timeout to change the jersey. It worked for one game; then they made it illegal."

Murphy remembers a 1959 game in which Redskins owner George Preston Marshall was tipped off that the Browns planned to wear a lighter, aluminum cleat on their shoes.

"He complained to the officials and made us change all the cleats on the field," he said.

Before joining the Browns, Murphy was trainer for the New York Yankees of the All-America Football Conference. He could have gone to work for the more famous baseball Yankees during the years of Mickey Mantle and Roger Maris, but he chose to stay in Cleveland.

"On the first day of training camp when we first went into the NFL in 1950, Paul told the boys, 'I would like us to become the New York Yankees of the baseball world and the Joe Louis of the fighting world.'"

After hearing that, Murphy felt there was no need to leave.

CHAPTER 2

The 1960s

ART MODELL

A rthur B. Modell was 35 years old when he put himself in hock and purchased the Cleveland Browns in 1961, virtually sight unseen, for the unheard-of sum of $3.925 million.

He was 37 when he fired Paul Brown for reasons amounting to "my survival or his survival." Two football seasons later, Modell's Browns captured the world championship.

Thus began a wild ride of fame and fortune for the only son of a Brooklyn, New York, middle-class couple.

Forced to drop out of school at the age of 14 when his father, George, died on a business sales trip in Austin, Texas, Modell rose from New York television advertising executive to National Football League mover and shaker. Along the way, he married a Hollywood actress named Patricia Breslin and was twice wooed for state political office, which he declined.

After the 1964 championship—Cleveland's last for a major professional sports team—Modell basked in the glory and

Art Modell (r) with Brian Sipe (Photo by Paul Tepley)

celebrity of NFL ownership for more than three decades. He was gregarious and humorous in public and an active civic leader.

But coaches and executives who worked for him saw a different side, an emotional, sometimes irrational, boss who constantly worried about his public image and meddled with his football operation.

"I really liked him," said Sam Rutigliano, Browns coach from 1978 to '84. "But you just never knew from day to day what was going to really happen. He would always come up with [suggestions] because he was always on the phone, talking to cronies, and all the owners fished out of the same pond.

"Art was the kind of guy that wanted everybody to like him. But he fell in and out of love fast."

Peter Hadhazy, Browns general manager in the 1970s, said, "He'd hear things at a cocktail party and come in the next day and ask, 'Why aren't we doing this?'"

Other than Blanton Collier, who succeeded Brown and coached eight years before hearing loss forced his retirement, no coach lasted longer than Rutigliano's six seasons under Modell.

"It was always hard because Art was at every practice and he was involved in everything," Rutigliano said. "The wins were absolutely exhilarating. After a win, he'd say, 'Let's go to Roman Gardens to eat.' The losses ... an example is he'd have his head on the desk and we'd be sitting there like a wake, waiting for somebody to say something."

Bill Belichick was Modell's coach the last five years he owned the Browns.

"Art had a pole. He wanted instant results because he thought of his age and his health and how much longer he was going to be in the game," Belichick said. "But at the same time, he wanted the youth and vigor of new faces and draft choices. He wanted the first-round draft choice to be an instant star to create and generate new interest and enthusiasm, kind of the marketing side of it.

"And he wanted to win the Super Bowl not 'this year' but 'today.' It's hard to balance that kind of newness and change. It was marketing and pizzazz versus fundamentally building a foundation and a solid team and organization. That was challenging."

Modell had numerous health problems over the years, but his humor helped him get through them. He had friendships with Hollywood stars, such as Jack Lemmon, Walter Matthau, Charlton Heston and Lucille Ball. Modell was a staunch Republican Party fundraiser and had the clout to host President Ronald Reagan and Secretary of State Henry Kissinger at Browns practices in the 1980s.

But few really understood what a poor businessman Modell was. Ultimately, the pressure of impending personal bankruptcy led him to do the unthinkable in November of 1995—sign a secret deal to move his franchise to Baltimore for the promise of greater stadium revenues.

Once hailed as the most powerful owner in the NFL, Modell traded it all ostensibly to be able to hand over his franchise to his wife and her two sons, David and John, whom Modell adopted after marriage. Modell was reviled in Cleveland and assailed nationwide like few figures in sports.

As he did after firing Brown, however, Modell overcame all odds and not only survived the national scorn, but saw his newly renamed Baltimore Ravens win the Super Bowl five years after his move.

Alas, insurmountable personal debt forced Modell to sell the franchise to a Baltimore businessman for $600 million. The Modells were out of football after the 2003 season. Another goal of Modell's—election to the Pro Football Hall of Fame—also seemed out of his grasp.

He never returned to Cleveland after his move.

BLANTON COLLIER

Blanton Collier once said the only head coaching jobs he would take were those with the University of Kentucky and the Cleveland Browns.

He succeeded coaching giants Paul (Bear) Bryant at Kentucky and Paul Brown in Cleveland. It took a humble man to succeed Brown, the architect and driving force of the Browns franchise from its inception.

Accepting the challenge cost Collier the friendship of Brown, who half-expected him to decline Art Modell's call after the brazen new owner shocked the football world and fired Brown in 1963.

"I can still picture his face filled with sadness when he came back from meeting with Paul," said Kay McLaughlin, Collier's daughter. "He told Art he wouldn't even consider the job until he talked with Paul. Paul initially said he had to take it. And then Paul's son, Mike, came to him in private and asked him not to do it.

"It was at that point that Daddy said, 'An era in our lives has passed.' As close as he was to Paul, he knew that Paul would never be able to forgive him.

"I think the loss of the friendship had to have been a terrible thing for both of them. I can't imagine as an adult losing that kind of friend."

Collier had been Brown's top assistant while the Browns' dynasty rolled from 1946 to 1953.

"He was the brains of our offense," said quarterback Otto Graham. "He did most of the coaching with me, frankly. Without him, we wouldn't have been as great as we were."

More than 30 years after Collier retired as coach and 20 years after he died, Graham joined a groundswell movement to have Collier inducted into the Pro Football Hall of Fame.

In his letter of endorsement, Graham wrote before he died, "Paul Brown may have been the Cleveland Browns' brain-trust, but Blanton Collier was our heart."

McLaughlin said her father succeeded in following two legends by being himself.

Collier described himself as a teachaholic and a coacha-holic. Don Shula said there hasn't been another teacher and technician to come along as good as Collier. Former players and coaches said Collier could teach any position on the field better than any position coach.

Blanton Collier (Photo by Paul Tepley)

Monte Clark, an offensive tackle on the Browns' last championship team of 1964, said that Collier gave his team a "superiority complex."

"Because of his cutting-edge special knowledge, we had confidence that we knew just a little more than others, and that everyone not using our technique didn't quite know how to do it the right way," Clark said.

Collier's sensitivity, understanding, and positive, upbeat style contrasted sharply with the stern and demanding rule under Brown. He opened up the Browns' offense and allowed Jim Brown to reach his pinnacle.

It is no coincidence that Brown had three of his four highest season rushing totals in the years with Collier as head coach.

When Collier steered the Browns to the 1964 NFL championship with a 27-0 upset victory of the Baltimore Colts, he validated Modell's daring move to fire Brown.

"Not only was it vindication of Art's decision, it was also vindication for the family," McLaughlin said. "Daddy was not a person who tooted his own horn. So to see him finally publicly recognized, it was very, very exciting. You know, he didn't get Coach of the Year that year."

McLaughlin still remembers her father's reaction the morning after winning the championship.

"He came downstairs early, as always, and got the paper, and he opened the paper with the great, big headline that said '27 to 0' and he had this big grin on his face and he said, 'Score's still the same,'" she said.

Unbeknownst to most, Collier was gradually going deaf.

"Many people didn't even know about it because he taught himself to lip-read at a very young age," McLaughlin said. "It was discovered in the navy. When they tested him, they found he had only 30 percent hearing.

"We knew that Daddy's hearing was getting worse and we all were amazed that he was able to do so much for so many years. Art tried everything. Not many people were aware how Art researched doctors and treatment to try and save Daddy's hearing."

Collier literally turned over the reins of the team to assistant coach Nick Skorich during a dismal 6-2 loss to the Dallas Cowboys in the next to last game in 1970. He could not hear the roar of 75,000 fans in Cleveland Municipal Stadium that day.

JIM BROWN

The name Jim Brown conjures images of an unstoppable force, 235 pounds of toughness breaking gang tackles and outrunning men 40 pounds lighter. He had the brute strength of a fullback, the moves and quickness of a halfback.

"He didn't need any blocking. He'd run over people," said guard Gene Hickerson.

"I have never seen a ballplayer in my life where every play was 100 percent all out. He never coasted on a play," said tackle Dick Schafrath.

"Anybody that's ever played with him or against him will tell you he's by far the best running back ever," said linebacker Vince Costello.

The accolades for Brown multiply over time. Nearly 40 years after Brown walked away from professional football in his prime at age 29, he remains a dominant figure in the sport. He is the conscience of the running back position, the standard by which all players who followed him are measured.

"The way I look at my career has not changed, and because of that it has allowed me to function very well," Brown said. "You give credit to everybody that does well, and you let nobody take away what you know you did."

Most of Brown's records have been broken due to changes in the game and the fact he played only nine seasons. His rushing total of 12,312 yards has been surpassed by six backs, but Brown's rushing average of 5.22 yards per carry still stands as the all-time record.

"Jamal Lewis of Baltimore had a great year [in 2003]," Brown says with a chuckle. "I see he had 2,066 yards. But then I look at his average and it was 5.3. The year I had 1,863 [in 14 games in 1963], my average was 6.4."

In the continuum of Browns history, Brown was the bridge from Paul Brown and Otto Graham to Art Modell and Blanton Collier.

In 1957, Brown sought to replace the retired Graham with Len Dawson or John Brodie in the draft. They were gone by Brown's choice at No. 6. He settled for the running back from Syracuse.

Their relationship was never warm. Paul Brown's fear tactics did not work on Jim Brown. The coach also was wary of Jim Brown's independent nature and intellect.

Said Mike Brown, Paul's son, "The point I would make about that relationship is with all its strains, they existed. I think they both recognized they were better off that way."

But when Modell, the brash new owner, clashed with the team's founding coach, Jim Brown encouraged a change. He welcomed Collier taking over.

"There were a lot of politics going on," Jim Brown said. "You had to deal with [Brown's racial] quota system, things that were going on at that time that were a little uncomfortable. Paul

Jim Brown (Photo by Paul Tepley)

didn't want to make certain changes. It was always enjoyable, but it became truly enjoyable with Blanton's attitude."

In three years with Collier as head coach, Brown averaged 1,617 yards, 5.6 a carry, and 12 touchdowns. He won his only NFL championship in 1964 and his second league MVP award in 1965.

And then he walked away to pursue a second career in acting. On the set of the motion picture *The Dirty Dozen,* in London, Brown reacted to Modell's ultimatum to report to training camp by announcing his retirement.

"I was basically finished, but I told Blanton I would think about coming back," Brown recalled. "Art kind of jumped the gun and went through a lot of things and took all possibility away."

Brown's acting career ran its course in the 1980s, though he continued to appear in movies. In 1988, he began focusing much of his energy on Amer-I-Can, a program that assists gang members and ex-convicts.

"These people care about being cared about. Most of them are looking for that. I know I was as a kid," he said.

Brown's father deserted him shortly after he was born. Brown was in his 40s when his father died. He refused to attend his funeral.

As a player, Brown forwarded the cause of economic freedom for African-American athletes. His athletic and acting careers did not make him wealthy, but rich.

"I wouldn't trade my life for anybody's," Brown said. "One of the nicest feelings I have in my life at this time is hearing from fans talking about their fathers talking about and respecting my game. That's one of the high points of having played.

"The greatest thing is having played during a time of racial strife and to develop these friendships and to have won a championship with an overachieving team. The respect is so high among the guys on that team and the quality of friendships. And the championship, that cemented it."

PAUL WARFIELD

Paul Brown was still being paid as a consultant a year after being fired as head coach. One of his lasting contributions in this capacity was to recommend that the Browns select Paul Warfield of Ohio State in the 1964 draft.

Brown saw Warfield as a much-needed injection of speed in the Browns' defensive secondary. Coach Blanton Collier agreed. Warfield was a 60-minute player at Ohio State and earned more notoriety as a cornerback than as a running back.

So when the Browns tabbed Warfield as their first-round pick, everyone, including Warfield, figured his NFL future was at cornerback.

"The date that changed was one spring day at Lakewood High School," Warfield said.

Unofficially, it may have been the first NFL minicamp. The Browns were still a progressive organization in the 1960s, ahead of the curve on such training innovations. Collier gathered all his rookies for a one-day indoctrination that included physicals, classroom sessions and an informal practice on the high school field.

"I was asked to spend some time on the defensive side, taking stances, movement, covering, and then I was asked to go on the offensive side because they just wanted to see what I looked like and moved like," Warfield said.

Collier stood next to Dub Jones, his offensive coordinator and a former Browns player, and watched Warfield run a pass pattern.

"I did something against a defender," Warfield recalled. "I can't remember specifically what it was, but the very first time I ran against a defender, I caught a ball and Blanton said, 'That's it. You're a receiver.'"

Collier's keen analytical eye paved the way for Warfield to become the most explosive and graceful receiver in Browns history.

When Warfield drove the 12 miles from his home in Warren, Ohio, to his first training camp at Hiram College, he did not realize the education awaiting him.

Ray Renfro, who had retired the year before as the Browns' all-time receptions leader, was invited by Collier to serve as Warfield's personal tutor.

"I was a receiver who knew absolutely nothing," Warfield said. "So many of these young players think it's all speed, quickness, explosiveness, strength—which is all a part of it. But those who attain monumental success are the ones who have insights and who know what to look for, who understand the game and are thinking players.

"That's what Ray passed on to me."

Warfield made an immediate impact. He led the team in receptions and touchdown catches his rookie season as the Browns won the NFL championship. Three times in his first six years Warfield averaged more than 20 yards a catch.

And then the Browns traded him.

In January of 1970, the Browns swapped Warfield, one of the most popular players in their history, to the Miami Dolphins for the third pick in the draft. They used it to select Purdue quarterback Mike Phipps.

Paul Warfield (Photo by Paul Tepley)

"It was a jolt, really," Warfield said more than 30 years later. "I was in the sixth year of my career and just came off an All-Pro season. The team was doing well. My career was going well.

"I was told personally by Art Modell. I was in a business meeting in Akron, Ohio. He was able to locate me and we talked for a very short period of time. He expressed regret that the decision was made. I have to admit going to Miami was not a place I desired to go."

In truth, the trade enhanced Warfield's Hall of Fame credentials. The Dolphins made it to the Super Bowl three years in a row and won two.

Warfield did not return to Cleveland in a Miami uniform until the 1973 season. The normal electricity of a Monday night game was turned up a notch for Warfield's arrival.

Warfield considers his introduction that night as one of the highlights of his career.

"When the opposing team is introduced, from the first player to the last, there is a usually a round of boos," he said. "When I was introduced, there was a roar and a standing ovation. It was exhilarating and emotional. Even Don Shula came over to me and mentioned that he was moved by that. That will stand out in my mind for as long as I'm alive."

Warfield left the Dolphins for the World Football League in 1975, and then returned to the Browns in 1976 at the age of 34.

He retired after two more seasons. He worked in various capacities with the Browns after his playing days. In 1998, he joined former teammate Calvin Hill as the front men of an ownership group that tried to buy the expansion Browns.

DICK SCHAFRATH

Dick Schafrath once ran 62 miles nonstop from Cleveland to Wooster to win a bet. He paddled 78 miles across Lake Erie in a canoe. He wrestled a bear. He served four four-year terms as Ohio senator for the 19th District.

But the scariest time he ever had?

"Watching game films with Paul Brown," he said. "There was a fear I had about him, a respectful fear. He'd single out people on each play when we'd watch the game films. If he'd single out your name many times, you weren't around."

Schafrath impressed the Browns' coach the first time they spent time together—at his first weigh-in as a rookie.

Brown was always fond of Ohio State players, and he drafted Schafrath in the second round in 1959 knowing he had to pack on a lot more weight to play left tackle for the Browns. Schafrath surprised the coach when he stepped on the scale and weighed 250 pounds.

"He said, 'You don't look that heavy,'" Schafrath recalled. "He poked around my shoulders and discovered I had suspenders under my T-shirt. They were holding up a 25-pound iron jockstrap.

"Paul smiled and said, 'Anybody that wants to get on this team that bad, we've got to give him a chance. But you better get heavier, boy.'"

Schafrath dedicated the next year of his life to following Brown's advice. He reported to his second training camp at 275 pounds—without the iron jockstrap.

"That was a mega-year for me," he said. "My dad made me some weights with axles from the farm with cement on the ends. I was in every eating contest across the state. I ate water-

Dick Schafrath (Photo by Paul Tepley)

melons, hamburgers, eggs, chicken, and I'd eat to win. I never lost."

For the next 12 years, Schafrath anchored the Browns' offensive line. He made the Pro Bowl six times. The Browns had the NFL rushing champion in seven of the 12 years Schafrath was the left tackle.

"Jim Brown always called me the plowhorse, the bulldog or the mule," he said.

Schafrath's exploits off the field were characteristic of his competitive instinct.

"I love challenges," he said. "I'm pursuing life every day. I get into so many crazy things."

In the 1970s, Schafrath ran a canoe livery and campgrounds in Loudonville, Ohio. To help out a friend, he started wrestling Victor the Bear at sports shows.

"The owner of the bear knew the bear fell in love with me," he said. "Victor finally died before one show. The promoter asked me that night if I'd be the bear because they sold a lot of tickets. So I put the bear costume on and had two of my kids lead me to the stage. I could hardly breathe. I about died."

Schafrath came by his political career by accident. While pursuing a land deal in Wyoming one day in 1985, he received a call from a friend to return to Ohio to interview for a vacant seat in the Ohio senate. He was appointed the next day, and then won re-election three times.

Schafrath retired from the senate in January of 2003 at the age of 66. In recent times, he has battled heart problems and cancer.

"I've got a pacemaker and a fibrillator," he said. "I was helping [Ohio State coach] Jim Tressel at a football camp and it went off three times. I've got to watch what I'm doing any more."

GENE HICKERSON

Leading his trademark sweep for Hall of Fame rushers Jim Brown, Bobby Mitchell and Leroy Kelly earned Gene Hickerson numerous honors as a Browns guard from 1958 through 1974.

Everyone remembers No. 66 pulling in front of the great Cleveland backs. But few fans knew the eccentricities of this private man.

"He's a wacko guy, always a contrarian," said former offensive line teammate Monte Clark. "But he was a hell of a football player."

Doug Dieken was a wide-eyed rookie as Hickerson's career was winding down. He said Hickerson was the first player to lug his own window air conditioner to his dorm room at Hiram College at training camp.

"Gene was a strange duck. He would do anything for you, but he had his own mannerisms. He liked to pull people's chains," Dieken said.

Thus, when word occasionally trickled out that Hickerson was a boyhood friend of rock 'n' roll legend Elvis Presley, some thought it another inside gag spread by Hickerson. But it was absolutely true.

Hickerson met Elvis through a high school football teammate in Memphis named Red West, who eventually became an influential member of Elvis's inner circle, called the Memphis Mafia.

Their friendship lasted until Elvis's death. Hickerson visited Elvis at Graceland, joined him on overnight trips to Las Vegas on his private jet and routinely sent him copies of Browns game films. Elvis was a big fan of Jim Brown and regarded the Browns as his favorite team.

Gene Hickerson (Photo by Paul Tepley)

"He wanted to play sports so bad," Hickerson said. "If he had started younger he could have, because he was no midget, you know. After he hit the big time, he formed a league in Memphis of two-handed touch football. There were 44 teams, and he paid for it all."

Hickerson has plenty of stories of Elvis's generosity.

"He used to hang around car dealers because he loved cars," he said. "He paid for a lot of cars for elderly people.

"I'll tell you what was amazing. About a year before he passed away, I'm at his place and in this big garage are these huge plastic sheets to protect cars from the heat. And I look under them and there are 13 Cadillacs under those sheets. I said, 'Elvis, what are you going to do with 13 Cadillacs?' He laughed and said, 'I don't know. You want one? Take one.'

"He had a big airplane with four engines, and one night we went over his house and he just said, 'C'mon, we're going to Las Vegas.' You know, he grew up with nothing like myself, and he enjoyed himself.

"One time I said, 'My mother is dying to meet you.' My mother lived only a short block from him, and he came over and he just sat there and talked and had Pepsi all night."

Hickerson played 14 seasons, missing one with a broken leg. His 202 games played rank fourth on the franchise's all-time list. He was the best guard of his time, a Pro Bowl selection six straight years.

"Every week he faced guys like Bob Lily, Merlin Olsen, Alex Karras—the best defensive tackle on every opponent," said receiver Gary Collins.

Clark played next to Hickerson on the Browns' awesome offensive line for five seasons. He said Hickerson was the best pulling guard in NFL history.

"The guy was incredible," Clark said. "He could run like a deer and he had excellent size for that time. He could go all year and not get beat on a pass. And when he pulled, his man was on the ground. Show me somebody else like that and I'll kiss your rear."

Despite these plaudits and numerous others from opponents who have gone to bat for him, Hickerson's final sweep—to the Pro Football Hall of Fame—has not been executed.

At 68 and a successful businessman since early in his playing days, Hickerson tries to feign indifference towards the eternal Hall of Fame debate that swirls around him.

"I could give a rat's ass," he dismisses. "I don't kiss anyone's ass. I know there are many ballplayers in the Hall of Fame that played four, five, six years. What did they do in six years that I didn't do in 14?"

He was told that eventually he will get in.

"Then I may not accept," he grumbled, adding, "It depends on what kind of mood I'm in."

FRANK RYAN

There is nobody better qualified to explain the intricacies of the complex quarterback rating system used in the NFL today than Frank Ryan.

He quarterbacked the Browns to their last NFL championship in 1964 while completing requirements for his Ph.D. in mathematics from Rice University.

And yet, "I have no idea how those are derived," Ryan said of the formula created to rank quarterbacks of different eras. "Quite frankly, I think it's easy to have great statistics like some of my contemporaries did, but they never won the big one.

Frank Ryan (Photo by Paul Tepley)

"I think even the presumption to rank the greatest quarterbacks of all time is unfair to the quarterbacks and to the sport. It's just not something that should be done."

Ryan played six seasons for the Browns in the 1960s and still ranks in the top five in most passing categories on the franchise's all-time list. For the record, his career rating of 81.4 is third.

He is the last quarterback—and the only one other than Otto Graham—to take the Browns all the way. He outplayed Hall of Famer Johnny Unitas in the 1964 title game, throwing three touchdowns to Gary Collins in leading the seven-point underdog Browns to a 27-0 victory.

"He didn't have that quick release, but, boy, he could throw," recalled Collins. "And Frank was a tough guy. I don't know if you knew that. When he took off to run, he was tough. He was 6'3", 210 pounds, maybe more."

Ryan's fascination with mathematics was evident to his teammates.

"Football really wasn't Frank's calling. Football was below him, the guy was so smart," Collins said.

Ryan was a backup quarterback who carried an academic major in physics at Rice University. He was accepted at graduate schools at UCLA and Cal-Berkeley, but decided to give his athletic career a longer look when Los Angeles Rams general manager Pete Rozelle—the future NFL commissioner—drafted him in the fourth round in 1958.

Ryan was acquired by the Browns in 1962 to serve as Jim Ninowski's backup. He took over as the starter after Ninowski suffered a broken collarbone in the eighth game and held the job until 1968.

"He was one of the brightest guys you'll ever see in pro football," said tackle Monte Clark. "He called his own plays. I think that his intelligence was a big advantage for us."

Linebacker Jim Houston said, "Can you imagine the brainpower that guy has?"

Ryan always defused the notion that his mathematical mind aided his athletic career. "It didn't help me avoid any interceptions, I know that," he said.

Ryan quips that he doesn't even remember the title of his doctoral thesis. It was "Characterization of the Set of Asymptotic Values of a Function Holomorphic in the Unit Disc."

"He was a genius in mathematics," remembered linebacker Vince Costello. "I used to play gin with him all the time. He was good in gin because he could remember everything well. We still have a running game going. We haven't played in 20 years, but he's still got a piece of paper in his pocket saying where we stand.

"He'd like to do way-out, stupid things. For instance, he took a picture once of throwing the ball left-handed and the photographer didn't know the difference. Frank thought it was a big deal he got it in the paper."

Ryan taught a mathematics class at Rice while an active player. After his playing career, he became athletic director at Yale University of the Ivy League, and then joined the administrative staff at Rice as a professor in mathematics.

Now retired, Ryan spends his days "in the backwoods of Vermont," tending to gardens, fishing his pond and doing independent data analysis for "six to eight hours a day" on his home computer.

"I'm continually fulfilling myself with my projects," Ryan said. "They are intellectual pursuits that are appealing to me, extremely hard problems and things that just keep me going."

Ryan said he believes there is only "one true statistic" to measure a quarterback, and that is the number of passes thrown for every touchdown pass.

"That ratio is probably the most important, in terms of quarterback effectiveness," he said.

Not surprisingly, his ratio of one touchown every 13 passes is the best in Browns history. Ryan knew that, of course.

GARY COLLINS

The offensive hero of the last Browns NFL championship in 1964 doesn't want to talk about his three touchdowns or anything about the game.

"I played in a ton of [bleeping] games after that and had great seasons, but I'm remembered for one thing," Collins said of catching three Frank Ryan passes for scores in the Browns' 27-0 upset of the Baltimore Colts.

"It's like Bobby Thompson. I've talked to him. He's so pissed off about talking about that home run. That's all people remember. He had a great batting average over his career. In my case, it's the '64 championship. That's all people want to talk about for 40 years, like it's the only game I ever played."

What would Collins rather be known for?

"I had a good career, not great," he said. "I made some big catches, had some big games. I was there when they needed me. I was that guy. Third down. First downs. Big catches. That was me. That was my job. That's what I did."

He did it better than any wide receiver in Browns history. His 331 career catches trail only the 662 posted by tight end Ozzie Newsome. Collins's 70 touchdowns are the most of any

Gary Collins (Photo by Paul Tepley)

Browns receiver. Only backs Jim Brown (126) and Leroy Kelly (90) had more.

Collins also doubled as the team's punter for six seasons. He led the NFL in 1965 with a gross average of 46.69 yards per punt.

But while he was a storied player, Collins became a stranger to the franchise after his retirement in 1971. He retreated to the insurance business in Hershey, Pennsylvania, seldom to be heard from. His return visits to Cleveland were as infrequent as his dropped passes.

"I have another life," he said in 2003. "When I retired, [former owner] Art Modell never said shit about me. Never said goodbye. Nobody from the Cleveland Browns organization even said, 'See ya.' I was bitter for a couple years, but, hell, I'm 62 years old and I've got four granddaughters and who gives a shit? As long as you can breathe."

Such orneriness was always a part of Collins's makeup. He said he was an angry player who often picked fights with teammates in practice.

"I had a bad marriage," he said of his playing days. "My best year in football was '66. I was separated the whole year, and she was living with a guy who I tried to work with. I was living in agony.

"It motivated me to be pissed off, and I took it out on football. It made me a good player in a game, but not in practice. I didn't want to be there. I set a bad example, looking back. But they knew that I wouldn't let them down."

For that reason, Collins was loved by his teammates.

"He was probably the best guy I played alongside of throughout my entire career," said Paul Warfield.

"A great receiver and just a great individual," said Kelly. "Most of the time, Gary was a good-humored person. I never really saw him get into it, except when Frank wouldn't get him the ball."

Collins was a confident player. His bold comments to the media often caught the attention of coach Blanton Collier, but he usually backed them up.

"The tougher the game, the looser I was," Collins said. "I'd tell them in the huddle, 'Don't worry about it. I'll pull you guys through.'

"A guy wrote a statistic one time that the number of balls I dropped probably don't go past three hands or two hands. And the guy that replaced me, Frank Pitts, he dropped more in two games than I did in my career.

"I dropped three in one game with broken ribs in a sleet storm. We lost to Dallas, 6-2, in the sleet and rain, and I got booed. That's when I gave the crowd the bird."

The Browns were 7-6-1 in Collins's first season of 1962 and 7-7 in his last of 1971. In the seven years in between, their record was 69-27-1 and they played in four NFL championship games, winning one.

"I had a hell of a run," Collins said.

JIM HOUSTON

Lin Houston, an offensive guard with the original Browns, was one of only two players to play for Paul Brown at Massillon Washington High School, Ohio State and the Cleveland Browns.

So Brown had to be looking out for Lin's younger brother, Jim, when he came of age and graduated from Ohio State in 1959.

"Paul sent me a little postcard: Are you interested in professional football?" Houston said. "I wrote 'yes' and sent it back. That's all I heard from him. Meanwhile, I was wined and dined and danced by San Francisco and several other teams. I had my bags packed for San Francisco."

By virtue of losing to the 49ers, 21-20, late in the 1959 season, the Browns jumped one spot ahead of them in the draft order. Brown made Houston his No. 1 pick, fifth overall, in 1960.

"It probably had a lot to do with knowing Lin and the family," Houston said. "But I don't think he ever said five words to me the whole time I played for him."

By the time he reported to the Browns as a rookie, Houston already had earned his license as an insurance agent. It came in handy. In one of Brown's first addresses to the team, the coach lectured, "You're going to be off Monday and Tuesday. Get a job."

Houston was an accomplished insurance salesman during his playing days and stayed in the profession for more than 40 years.

When Blanton Collier succeeded Brown in 1963, the new coach moved the 240-pound Houston from defensive end to outside linebacker. He made the Pro Bowl four times and was a starter on the 1964 team that shocked the Johnny Unitas-led Baltimore Colts, 27-0, to win the NFL championship.

"We had a collective attitude that nobody was going to beat us," Houston said. "That is a remarkable feeling with an athletic team because you depend on each other and you will react to them. You're going to make sure to carry out your responsibility so that you don't let your teammates down."

Of all the great coaches Houston played for, none was comparable to Ohio State's Woody Hayes.

"If something wasn't going right at practice, he would go into his harangue of swearing and would tear his cap in two," Houston said. "That would get our attention. It happened a lot.

"One day the equipment manager caught Woody in his private room and he was snipping the strings in his hat. So he knew in advance what he was going to do if there was a lull in practice. That was Woody Hayes—prepared for everything."

VINCE COSTELLO

How does a man who played only six-man football in high school and was not drafted by the NFL go on to start at middle linebacker on the 1964 Browns championship team?

For Vince Costello, it was all a matter of perfect timing.

After playing four years at Ohio University, Costello was invited to Browns training camp in 1956 by defensive coordinator Howard Brinker. He arrived with a badly pulled hamstring injury suffered earlier playing minor league baseball for the Cincinnati Reds.

"My leg was black and blue from the bottom of my ankles to the top of my butt," Costello said. "One day Paul Brown called me in and said, 'I don't think you're gonna make it with that leg. Why don't we get you a coaching job and you come back next year?'"

Costello took him up on the raincheck and retreated to coach at Big Walnut High School that year. "We didn't win a game," he said.

The Browns also had a bad year in 1956—their first losing season. In the middle of the year, Brown joined the growing trend and copied the NFL-champion New York Giants' 4-3 defensive alignment. It was the first time Brown abandoned his famed five-man defensive front.

When Costello returned to Browns camp in 1957, he found two startling things—rookie No. 1 pick Jim Brown ("You could just see he was great right away," he said) and Paul Brown had a new task for him. Brown lined him up at middle linebacker on the first day. Costello was a fixture in the middle of the defense for the next 10 years.

Not a bad career for a kid who never played regular football in high school.

Growing up in Magnolia, Ohio, Costello joined a group of kids who protested the local school board for not fielding a football team. Authorities were mindful of the costs of starting up a football program. They compromised by instituting six-man football.

"We just took what we could get," Costello said. "That was a challenging sport. We played on a field 40 yards wide and 80 yards long. You'd have two ends, a center, two halfbacks and a quarterback, and two guys had to handle the ball on every play. I was quarterback. Everything else was the same as regular football, except you'd begin every series first and 15.

"On defense, you'd have two ends, a nose guard and three defensive backs. I'd play safety. It wasn't a whole lot different than middle linebacker. It was open field, a lot of running."

Costello was one of Brown's biggest fans—even after the team hit the skids and teammates lobbied for a coaching change to Blanton Collier. When Brown formed his second franchise, the Cincinnati Bengals, Costello joined him as linebackers coach.

PAUL WIGGIN

In 1956, Paul Wiggin never expected to be drafted by, of all teams, the Cleveland Browns. The native of Modesto, California, still had a year of eligibility left at Stanford University.

But Paul Brown exercised a "future" pick and took the defensive tackle in the sixth round. Wiggin joined the Browns the following year as a member of the draft class that included Jim Brown.

Wiggin was moved to defensive end and never missed a game over 11 seasons.

"If someone said, 'Paul Wiggin, you're 21 years old and it's 1957 and you can go anywhere you want,' I'd say I want to play in Cleveland," Wiggin said 35 years after he retired. "It was the greatest city to play football in. We won every year. We were very close. I loved the Cleveland Browns."

Wiggin had a love-hate relationship with the tyrannical Brown that was typical of the players on those teams.

"I don't know that I ever hated anybody, but if I ever disliked somebody it was Paul Brown, at times, in my career," he said.

"But one time after a game, Paul Brown put his hand on my shoulder and said, 'Thanks.' I had tears in my eyes.

"That was one of the most meaningful things. If I live to be 100, I'll never forget that. What that told me was he was special in my life. I vividly remember telling my wife that I didn't want to play for anybody else.

"He didn't want you to like him when you played for him. Then, when you retire and you're not there any more and you need anything, Paul Brown was always there for you, like you wouldn't believe."

Wiggin learned of Brown's lasting influence after he retired and went into coaching.

He joined the San Francisco 49ers as defensive line coach and then was promoted to defensive coordinator. He got his big break in 1975 when he was named to replace the legendary Hank Stram as head coach of the Kansas City Chiefs.

"When things got a little shaky, I asked them, 'Why in the heck did you hire me?' And they said, 'Because Paul Brown said you'll be a good coach.' That's how powerful he was in the game of football in those days."

Wiggin was one of the many players who supported the firing of Brown after the 1962 season.

"I thought there were some things that had gone on with our football team from the standpoint of time passing things by, particularly the play-calling aspect," he said. "If I had a choice, I wish Paul Brown would have brought in and believed in a coaching staff to do some more things for him, because the game was evolving."

Wiggin was the starting left defensive end on the 1964 Browns team that shocked the heavily favored Baltimore Colts, 27-0, and won the NFL championship.

"If I remember any one thing it would be that [linebacker] Galen Fiss played a perfect football game," Wiggin said. "I've been in football all my life and I've never seen a perfect game since."

ERICH BARNES

Erich Barnes was one of the hardest hitters of his day. The big cornerback was considered a dirty player by Browns fans—

until he joined the Browns in a trade in 1965.

"It's just a matter of geographical location," Barnes said of his image, laughing. "No one in New York ever called me dirty.

"I was a little bit ahead of my time when it came to my style of play. I was a big defensive back, 6'3" and 210 pounds, and there weren't many around then. And I was fast for my size.

"I felt being aggressive was the way to play. Now, everybody tries to play that way."

Opposing fans considered Barnes a headhunter because he tackled high.

"I think that was unfair," he said. "I never tried to hit anybody in the face or in the head. I liked to tackle high, because with my size I wanted to get my shoulders and hands on the guy. Because of that, guys went down relatively hard."

Barnes disdains the blind-shot helmet hits he sees so rampant in today's NFL.

"We didn't use our helmet too much in my day," he said. "Tackling, to me, is an art. Your head wasn't designed to give a blow. It was to absorb a blow.

"In 14 years, I never got a headache making a tackle. I don't remember missing that many, either. You see a lot of those helmet hits now. I'm a defensive player and I like aggressive play, but whenever I see a tackle where you can get hurt, that's the play I don't like. That's the way they're teaching nowadays."

Barnes was a fourth-round draft choice of the Chicago Bears in 1958. At Purdue University, one of his defensive coaches was George Steinbrenner, now the boss of the New York Yankees.

"He was a good football man," Barnes said. "I still bump into him on the banquet circuit and call him now and then and wish him good luck."

Barnes also played for the New York Giants, but seven of his 14 NFL seasons were spent with the Browns. The Browns played in three NFL championship games in that span, losing each time.

His first return to Cleveland after retiring was to see the last game in old Cleveland Municipal Stadium in 1995. Barnes said he comes back to see one or two games every year in the new stadium.

BILL NELSEN

The greatest trade the Browns ever made with the Pittsburgh Steelers brought them Bill Nelsen for Dick Shiner in 1968. The swap of quarterbacks worked out so heavily in Cleveland's favor that the teams have not traded since.

Nelsen was 27 when he came to the Browns, his knees already surgically repaired four times. He was supposed to serve as Frank Ryan's backup. But when Ryan struggled in the first three games in 1968, coach Blanton Collier made the switch to Nelsen.

Nelsen held the starting job for four seasons. In Pittsburgh, Shiner played two years and won three games for the Steelers. Nelsen's first appearance came against the Steelers of coach Bill Austin. He won that game and six of eight against his former team.

"One of my great thrills was to go into Pittsburgh one time and see a big bedsheet hanging on the wall that said, 'Thanks Bill Austin, for Bill Nelsen,'" Nelsen said 30 years after he retired.

It didn't take long for Nelsen to establish his leadership ability. He won nine of his first 11 games and then orchestrated a playoff win over Dallas.

But in the biggest game Nelsen was to play, the Browns were shut out by Baltimore, 34-0, for the NFL championship. The Colts went on to play the AFL champion New York Jets in Super Bowl III, which came to be regarded as one of the most important games in pro football history.

"It was just another game," Nelsen said of the newly renamed Super Bowl. "Then it just got bigger and bigger. The hype of it now, I don't know if I could play in the game. I'd be too nervous to go out there."

Under Nelsen, the Browns came up one victory short of the Super Bowl two times—in the 1968 season and again in 1969, when they lost to Minnesota, 27-7.

The following year, Nelsen led the Browns in a matchup against Joe Namath and the Jets in the first-ever *Monday Night Football* game.

"I bet it wasn't five or six years later that somebody said, 'You threw the first Monday night touchdown pass,'" Nelsen said. "I didn't know. It wasn't a big deal.

"I remember we stayed in the same hotel as the Jets that day, the Hollenden House downtown. We're going out the door and Namath's being swamped by all the fans for autographs, and I just walked through and nobody noticed me.

"We won, 31-21. My mother ended up writing a letter to [announcer] Howard Cosell saying, 'Do you know who won the game? All you talked about was Namath!'"

Nelsen's courage to play through the pain of his ravaged knees was inspirational to teammates.

"If you wanted to go to war with somebody, Bill Nelsen was the guy," said running back Leroy Kelly.

"The guy had no cartilage in his knees," said tackle Doug Dieken. "He'd get his knees drained the day before every game. I can remember going into the locker room and seeing [team physician] Doc Ippilito draining his knees and I'd almost pass out."

Nelsen attributed his success to a stellar surrounding cast that included Kelly, receivers Paul Warfield and Gary Collins, and tight end Milt Morin.

"One time Blanton called me in in the off season and we watched Namath throwing on film," Nelsen said. "Blanton talked to me about throwing the ball more to Paul. In those days, I threw maybe 25 times a game, and I had Gary and Leroy and Milt Morin to think about, too.

"Blanton just looked at me and said, 'Try to throw more to Paul.'"

The Browns traded Warfield in 1970 for the draft rights to quarterback Mike Phipps, Nelsen's successor. After the 1972 season, a fifth knee operation prompted Nelsen's retirement.

In his 60s, Nelsen said his knees are the least of his aches.

"The biggest thing I have is my neck and back areas are not real good," he said. "I can't turn very well. My spinal cord is crushed a little. I've got a lot of arthritic things in there from the days in Pittsburgh when I got hit a lot. Not in Cleveland."

LEROY KELLY

They say you leave the NFL the same way you enter it. A player's career typically comes full circle. Not so with Leroy Kelly.

He came to the Browns as a virtual unknown from Morgan State University, drafted in the eighth round of 20 in the last Cleveland championship season of 1964. He left as a

Hall of Famer, a worthy successor to Jim Brown on the team's incomparable chain of great running backs.

"I chalk it up as fate, with the Browns drafting me," Kelly said.

Neither Kelly nor the Browns considered him the heir to Brown when he was drafted. Kelly thought he'd play defensive back. But after coach Blanton Collier's rookie camp in May, Kelly was instructed to return in the summer 10 pounds heavier because he would compete at halfback.

Brown took a liking to Kelly, and the scared rookie made the team as a backup and kick return specialist. He scored on a 68-yard punt return in the championship season of 1964 and added two breakaway scoring runs in 1965, when he led the NFL in punt returns.

Brown was still in his prime, so Kelly carried the ball only 43 times in his first two seasons. One of Kelly's memorable highlights was starting in the backfield next to Brown against the Pittsburgh Steelers on a rainy Saturday night in front of 80,000 in Municipal Stadium.

Almost 40 years later, Kelly recalls the game vividly.

"Ernie Green was out with an injury," Kelly said. "It rained the whole game. We won in the last 20 seconds on a Frank Ryan pass to Gary Collins across the middle. I kind of set up that last drive with a couple of flare passes, one out to the right and one out to the left."

It was the first time the two future Hall of Fame backs played a whole game together—and the last.

The following summer, with his teammates sweating in training camp in Hiram, Brown stunned the sports world by announcing his retirement while in London filming *The Dirty Dozen*, his second motion picture.

"Thank the Lord," Kelly said in retrospect.

"We weren't ready for Jim Brown to retire," said Dick Schafrath, the left tackle. "We were in the middle of our careers. We were all coming together at the same time. We thought we'd be good forever."

Kelly stepped in and filled Brown's giant footsteps. He rushed for 1,141 yards and 15 touchdowns in '65, 1,205 yards and 11 touchdowns in '66, and 1,239 yards and 16 touchdowns in '67. The latter two seasons, Kelly led the NFL in rushing. He is the last Browns back to do that.

Kelly's rushing averages of 5.5 yards, 5.1 and 5.0 in that stretch compared favorably to those of Brown's the previous three seasons.

"When Jim retired, the excellent offensive line was still there," Kelly said. "With Gene Hickerson and Schaf, John Wooten, Monte Clark and John Morrow, they made it very easy for me."

Kelly played 10 seasons. When he retired in 1974, his 7,274 yards rushing ranked fourth on the NFL all-time list. Yet Brown's giant shadow cast down on him until he was elected to the Hall of Fame in 1994.

At the time, Wooten called it a special induction for the Browns' fabulous offensive line of the 1960s.

"We feel Jim could've made it with Mamby Pamby out there blocking," Wooten said. "We feel we're certainly a part of Kelly. We think Kelly's induction represents the Cleveland Browns system. That's why this one is so important to us."

CHAPTER 3

The 1970s

HOMER JONES

Homer Jones lost all mementos of his NFL career in a fire on his cattle farm in Pittsburg, Texas, in 1995.

But someone later sent him a videocasette of his only highlight as a Cleveland Brown—a 94-yard kickoff return for a touchdown to start the second half in the first ever game on ABC's *Monday Night Football*.

"I was just doing my job," he said.

Jones's arrival to the Browns in 1970 was steeped in controversy. He was the receiver tabbed to succeed Paul Warfield.

In fact, the very day that Warfield was traded to the Miami Dolphins for the draft choice the Browns used to select Purdue quarterback Mike Phipps, Jones was acquired from the New York Giants for three players.

Then 29, Jones had been one of the league's most dangerous deep receivers. He led the NFL in yards per catch in two of his five seasons as a Giants starter. He led the NFL with 13 touchdown catches in 1967.

He produced an immediate dividend in that 1970 season opener against the New York Jets.

The Jets, with Joe Namath, had put the American Football League on the map by upsetting the Baltimore Colts in Super Bowl III a year earlier. More than 85,000 fans jammed Cleveland Municipal Stadium for their arrival. It was the biggest sporting event in Cleveland since the 1964 NFL championship game. The attendance record will stand forever.

Jones's touchdown return to start the second half increased the Browns' lead to 21-7. They went on to upset Namath and the Jets, 31-21.

"[Guard] Al Jenkins told me to follow him and he'd take me to daylight," Jones recalled of his big play. "I told him, 'Don't stop. Keep going.' One of the biggest problems you get with linemen is they always want to stop and find someone to block. If they just keep moving, it works very well."

Jones was credited with being the first player to spike the ball after touchdowns. But he was unable to perform his signature spike after his touchdown return on national television because the ball was pried loose by a teammate in the celebration.

"I'm supposed to be the granddaddy of the spike," Jones said. "I had always said when I made my first touchdown, I was gonna do like Frank Gifford and Alex Webster and throw the ball in the stands.

"But in 1964, Pete Rozelle changed the rule. So I had my mind on throwing it to the stands; then when I crossed the goal line, I thought of the fine of $500. So I threw it to the ground. It got to be like a trademark."

Jones scored 38 touchdowns in his seven NFL seasons. The one in Cleveland is the only one he didn't celebrate by spiking the ball.

Jones still holds several Giants receiving records. His career average of 22.3 yards per catch remains an NFL record.

Jones scored only one other touchdown with the Browns in 1970. He retired after that season at the age of 30.

"I got real tired of running," he said.

MIKE PHIPPS

The NFL was changing fast in 1970, the first year of realignment following the merger with the American Football League.

The Browns, Pittsburgh Steelers and Baltimore Colts uprooted from the established NFL and agreed to join the old AFL teams in a newly created American Football Conference to balance the expanding league.

The Browns insisted the Steelers join them in the same division to continue their rivalry. Owner Art Modell envisioned the Browns dominating the new conference.

That year, the Steelers owned the first pick in the draft and selected quarterback Terry Bradshaw.

Seeking their own savior, the Browns shocked their fans by trading receiver Paul Warfield to the Miami Dolphins for the third pick in the draft. They used it to choose Mike Phipps.

Phipps, an All-American at Purdue University, was more highly rated than Bradshaw, who starred at little known Louisiana Tech.

Bradshaw would lead the Steelers out of mediocrity and to four Super Bowl championships in six years.

Phipps would go down as one of the Browns' all-time draft busts. He never escaped the giant shadow left by Warfield's departure.

"He just wasn't the horse for the course," said former general manager Pete Hadhazy. "Paul was such a popular guy and a great player, and that stigma hung over Phipps."

Phipps's best season was his first as the starter, when he led the Browns to the playoffs and nearly upset the Miami Dolphins in their perfect season of 1972. That was as good as it got for Phipps.

"I don't know if the pressure really did get to him," said offensive tackle Doug Dieken. "He wasn't one of those real intense competitors. I don't know if he ever had that real passion for it."

Phipps suffered in comparisons to the two charismatic leaders that quarterbacked the Browns before and after him—Bill Nelsen and Brian Sipe.

"Mike had as much ability as anybody," Nelsen said. "He could run like a deer, was strong, but passing-wise, his arm wasn't as good as the rest of his ability. The only thing I'd say about Mike is I think he'd rather have gone fishing than play football. Then you had Brian, who didn't have all that ability, and he became a winner."

Sipe's emergence allowed the Browns to trade Phipps in 1977 to Chicago for the Bears' No. 1 choice the following year. Ultimately, the Browns swapped that pick in 1978 to the Los Angeles Rams, who wanted to move up three notches to take Oklahoma running back Elvis Peacock.

The Browns then used the Rams' position at No. 23 to select Alabama receiver Ozzie Newsome.

Thus, Phipps's lasting claim to fame was that he was traded for not one but two future Pro Football Hall of Famers—Warfield coming in, and Newsome going out.

DOUG DIEKEN

When coach Nick Skorich called to inform Doug Dieken that he was drafted in the sixth round by the Browns in 1971, Dieken responded, "Nick who?"

"I thought the coach was still Blanton Collier," Dieken said.

Such cutting one-liners would become a staple of Dieken's repertoire as a popular charity banquet speaker and Browns radio and television analyst after his playing days ended. But he was not kidding when he spoke to Skorich that day.

"He got a little bothered by it. I asked him if there was any chance I could play tight end. He said, 'We'll see when you get here,'" Dieken recalled.

His conversion from tight end to offensive tackle was already a fait accompli. Despite having only one quarter playing experience in a college All-Star game at the position, Dieken would make a franchise-record 194 consecutive starts at left tackle through 1984.

He is also first on the Browns' all-time list with 203 consecutive games, second with 14 consecutive seasons played, and third with 203 total games played.

"I learned under fire," Dieken said. "There were times in my first training camp I would have 10 different defensive linemen after practice line up and take pass rushes at me.

"Bob McKay got hurt in the seventh game, so they sent me in for him. I grew up watching Gary Collins, Leroy Kelly and Gene Hickerson, those guys, and all of a sudden I'm in the huddle with them. I was just as excited as I could be until I went to the line of scrimmage and I saw [Atlanta Falcons All-Pro end] Claude Humphrey.

"That's when I learned to hold. It was a matter of survival."

Dieken proceeded to make a second career out of his self-deprecating humor. He drove a car with vanity license plates that read: ME HOLD. When he retired, friends at the Bay Village service department honored him by painting a yellow line at the front of his house heading east, with a yard for every yard he accumulated in holding penalties.

"It ended up in the cemetery down the road," Dieken said.

In the end, no player better appreciated the Browns' rivalry with the Pittsburgh Steelers than Dieken. His feuds with members of Pittsburgh's famed Steel Curtain were legendary. To this day, Dieken receives a card every Mother's Day signed by former Steelers lineman Dwight White.

"He used to think my first name was Mother," Dieken said.

One of Dieken's lasting regrets was never winning a game in Pittsburgh's Three Rivers Stadium. An individual highlight, though, was catching a touchdown pass from Paul McDonald on a fake field goal play in a 1983 game against Houston.

"I was always complaining that I should still be a tight end," Dieken said. "That play was designed to be a dumpoff to [kicker] Matt Bahr to get a first down. But I got so wide open, even McDonald couldn't miss me."

BRIAN SIPE

Years after Brian Sipe threw the most heartbreaking interception in any Browns game, former teammate and friend Jerry Sherk made an observation. Sherk was pursuing a graduate degree in psychology at the time.

"I kid him sometimes," Sherk says now. "I tell him, 'You really wanted to throw that interception, didn't you? You didn't want to get any more famous. You just wanted to go on and have a normal life.'"

Sipe had risen from 13th-round draft choice in 1972 to league MVP in 1980. He was demoted his first two seasons to the team's "taxi squad." He advanced from nearly being traded to one of the most popular players in team history.

When Pete Hadhazy joined the Browns as general manager in 1976, Sipe had no support inside the team.

"My first week with the Browns, I met with all the coaches and I said, 'Is there anybody on this team who thinks that Brian Sipe can take us to the Super Bowl?' To a man, they all said no," Hadhazy recalled. "No coach was opposed to us trying to move Brian if we could get anything for him."

But not even the expansion Seattle Seahawks would give up a draft choice for Sipe. A proposed trade fell through when Seattle drafted a quarterback instead.

An injury to Mike Phipps put Sipe on the field. After his third start, an embarrassing loss in Denver, Sipe was lambasted by Hadhazy in a postgame diatribe.

"As far as Brian Sipe is concerned, he has yet to prove he could play in the NFL," Hadhazy railed. The story was emblazoned across the top of *The Plain Dealer* sports page the next morning.

Sipe went on to set every Browns career passing record. He is the last Browns player to be named NFL MVP.

He was unassuming physically, barely six feet tall and not blessed with a strong arm. But Sipe had the intangibles that attracted teammates to follow him. His career took off when Sam Rutigliano became coach in 1978 and built an offense around Sipe's ability to lead.

Rutigliano said, "When Brian Sipe played, 10 guys on offense and everybody on defense felt we could win. If you could see him with three or four minutes to go—we're getting

Brian Sipe (Photo by Paul Tepley)

the crap beat out out of us by San Diego on a Monday night, and I'm calling timeouts and Brian says, 'Good for you, Sam. It's not over.' What a tremendous competitor."

Sipe was the rare kind of quarterback who inspired linemen to block better and receivers to catch anything thrown their way.

"He had that charisma," said left tackle Doug Dieken. "He made people believe that when he did something it was going to work. He was unbelievable that way."

Rutigliano's offense and Sipe's career all came together in the 1980 season, when the Browns won 11 games and unseated the mighty Pittsburgh Steelers as division champs. Sipe's last-second heroics accounted for repeated comeback victories. Cleveland fell in love with the unassuming quarterback with the boyishly handsome looks.

It was taken for granted that the Browns were going to the "Siper Bowl." And then came the fateful playoff loss to Oakland in minus-36 degree wind chill. The play remains frozen in time.

With 49 seconds left in the game, Rutigliano eschewed what would have been a 31-yard field goal try and called one more play. Sipe's pass for Ozzie Newsome from the Oakland 13 was intercepted in the end zone by Mike Davis. Oakland won, 14-12.

Rutigliano's career went downhill from there. He was skewered for not kicking the field goal.

More than 20 years later, Sipe said at a public dinner honoring Rutigliano, "I want you to know, Sam, that I let you down, because you trusted me."

But Sipe's popularity with the fans never abated, even after he defected to the fledgling United States Football League following the 1983 season.

"I just think he's part of the Cleveland legacy, and part of that legacy since the 1964 world championship is heartbreak," theorized Sherk. "I think the fans related to him first of all because he wasn't expected to do anything as a ballplayer. It really tied into the Cleveland population.

"Cleveland's an underrated place; the town's people are blue collar, and Brian had that attitude and just kind of melded. And he did a terrific job. He literally came in as a rookie that didn't know if he ever could play a few snaps in the NFL and ended up as the most valuable player. That's quite a transformation."

Peter Hadhazy

In 35 years of owning the Browns, Art Modell allowed only one person to hold the title of general manager. That was Peter Hadhazy.

Hadhazy, who came to America from Hungary at an early age, became acquainted with Modell while he worked in the NFL office in the late 1960s. Modell hired him as an executive vice president in 1976 and added general manager to his title the following year.

Hadhazy made an immediate splash in his first year when he reacquired Paul Warfield after the collapse of the rival World Football League. Warfield was 33 and over the hill, but Modell wanted to salve the PR scars left from the trade of Warfield in his prime six years earlier to the Miami Dolphins.

"Art was soothing the conscience of the fans and his own conscience, I guess, by bringing him back," Hadhazy said more than 25 years later. "It was as much a PR move as a competitive move, because that was in his twilight years."

When the WFL shut down, Hadhazy had his sights set on another future Hall of Famer, fullback Larry Csonka, who was 30 and still had tread on his tires.

"We came within an eyelash of signing Csonka," Hadhazy recalled. "The plan was to sign Csonka before the draft and then take the best offensive lineman in the draft, who was Pete Brock. I was dealing with Ed Keating, Csonka's agent from Cleveland.

"About two days before the draft, I gave Keating a proposal and he said he wouldn't look at anything until after the draft. I told him we couldn't wait. We were in desperate need of a fullback and we had to take Mike Pruitt.

"The Giants came in with an offer of guaranteed money and endorsements in New York for Csonka. When I saw Keating, I said, 'You dirty bastard.' Eddie said, 'They blitzed us.' I've told Larry the story and to this day he says Keating never told him of our offer."

Hadhazy was the Browns executive who unwittingly inspired Brian Sipe to great heights. Hadhazy tried to trade the unheralded quarterback prior to the 1976 draft. Failing that, he blasted Sipe after his third start, saying to reporters, "He has yet to prove he could play in the NFL."

It was the first example of Hadhazy's infamous temper.

The next morning, *The Plain Dealer* published a picture of Hadhazy yelling alongside the headline: "Browns GM says Sipe can't play in the NFL, says heads will roll."

"I called Sipe that morning after practice and apologized to him," Hadhazy said. "I felt a little trepidation going to practice, but Art insisted I go—the two of us go, as a sign of unity. When we got through the gate, Sipe grabbed me by the back of the collar and by the belt, and that kind of loosened all the tension.

"Here's the funny part. Every time Brian Sipe broke another one of Otto Graham's records, either Art Modell or [public relations chief] Nate Wallack or a player with the Browns would say, 'You were really right about Sipe.'

"I'd say, 'I'm responsible for him breaking these records. Look at how it tightened his ass up.'"

Hadhazy's other major contribution was hiring Sam Rutigliano as coach in 1978. Hadhazy left the Browns after the riveting 1980 season ended in the shocking playoff loss to Oakland.

"There were so many things Art and I were disagreeing on that we used to agree on," he said. "I felt Art didn't want a general manager. He wanted to be his own.

"There were great times and bad times, and it went back and forth. I hated him at times, but Art's basically a good, warm human being outside nine to five. Between nine to five, he's a bitch. He cares about people. He has empathy. But he chooses the people he cares about and he can love you one minute and hate you the next minute."

SAM RUTIGLIANO

Art Modell saw home attendance dropping and excitement waning in 1977. The last home game drew 30,898 to cavernous Cleveland Municipal Stadium—the second smallest crowd in Modell's tenure as Browns owner.

So when he conducted a search for his fifth head coach, college football legends Joe Paterno of Penn State and Ara Parseghian of Notre Dame were floated as candidates.

It was all a smokescreen.

Two weeks earlier, Peter Hadhazy, Modell's top lieutenant at the time, notified Sam Rutigliano that "unless you blow the interview, the job's going to be yours."

Sam Rutigliano (Photo by Paul Tepley)

Rutigliano, a native of Brooklyn, N.Y., had never been a head coach before. He was coaching quarterbacks and receivers for Hank Stram with the New Orleans Saints—his fourth pro team in 11 years.

The Saints promptly lost a game to the winless Tampa Bay Buccaneers.

The embarrassment of being the first victim of the 1976 expansion franchise after a record 26 straight losses gnawed at Rutigliano on the drive home with his wife Barbara.

"Isn't this unbelievable?" he said to her. "After 11 years, I finally have a chance and there's no way the Browns are going to be interested in me now."

He was wrong. Modell loved Rutigliano's engaging personality in the interview and hired him. Rutigliano provided the jolt of energy the Browns badly needed.

The Browns captivated the city with an exciting offensive team built around charismatic quarterback Brian Sipe. When the team faltered, Rutigliano's humor kept everyone entertained.

Beyond the laughs, though, was the making of a playoff contender. The Browns just missed in 1979 with a 9-7 record that earned Rutigliano AFC Coach of the Year honors.

Amid high hopes, the following season started with two losses. Then the Browns ran off 11 wins in their last 14 games. Most were last-minute thrillers that earned them the nickname Kardiac Kids.

By the time the Browns hosted the Oakland Raiders in the playoffs, a Super Bowl atmosphere intoxicated Cleveland.

The playoff meeting on a brutally cold January 4 day produced one of the franchise's all-time heartbreaking losses. It would be the beginning of the end for Rutigliano.

The coach took the blame for eschewing a 31-yard field goal on second down and calling "Red Right 88," a pass play from the Raiders' 13-yard line with the Browns behind, 14-12, in the final minute. Sipe's pass, intended for tight end Ozzie Newsome, was intercepted by Raiders safety Mike Davis with 49 seconds left.

The pass was supposed to go to Dave Logan crossing underneath from the left side, but Sipe saw Newsome open on the other side before he looked to Logan.

"The first read and the only read was Dave," Rutigliano recalled. "And if it wasn't there, Brian was to throw it to some blonde in the bleachers. Brian saw Ozzie open, doesn't have a strong arm to begin with, the weather was terrible, and the ball started floating.

"As I'm walking off the field and going through the [stadium] tunnel, I'm praying. Really, I'm praying, 'Keep your calm … don't say nothing, but don't say a lot.'"

The playoff game fell squarely in the middle of Rutigliano's run as coach. The Browns were 28-21 before it, and 19-31 after it.

The following year, the growing presence of substance abuse in the NFL inspired Rutigliano to form a confidential self-help group within his team called the Inner Circle. Rutigliano grew obsessed with the mission of saving a handful of players, most of whom were never identified, from poisoning their careers and lives with drugs.

As the losses mounted and the team became distracted, Rutigliano found himself in the position of defending his extracurricular activity as an unofficial life counselor. He was fired midway through the 1984 season after a loss to the Cincinnati Bengals, who were still operated by Modell nemesis Paul Brown.

Rutigliano attended the news announcement of his firing and then conducted his final meeting of the Inner Circle.

"It's interesting," he said to the players in the room, all recovering addicts. "You guys were all supposed to go before me, and now I'm going before you. I really feel good about all of you, about your chances of making it."

Rutigliano turned down an opportunity to coach the Buffalo Bills. When he realized "the only thing that really energized me was football," he accepted an invitation from the Rev. Jerry Falwell to coach at Liberty University. He retired from coaching in 2000 at the age of 67.

Through it all, Rutigliano continued to maintain his residence in suburban Waite Hill, Ohio.

JERRY SHERK

The year that Jerry Sherk's life changed, he was leading the NFL with 12 sacks through 10 games.

In the fourth game of the 1979 season, Sherk put on a show for ABC announcer Howard Cosell in a Monday night game against the undefeated Dallas Cowboys. He sacked quarterback Roger Staubach three times and recovered a fumble.

"He played the best game of any defensive lineman I ever saw," coach Sam Rutigliano said. "He controlled the entire middle of the line."

Life was so good. The defensive tackle was mounting a tremendous comeback in his 10th year after missing the previous season because of major knee surgery.

"I was all set to regain my stature," Sherk, a four-time Pro Bowler, recalled. "And then the staph infection hit."

At some point in the middle of the season, possibly in a game in St. Louis, Sherk developed a boil on an elbow. The following week, he scraped it on the artificial turf field of Veteran's Stadium in Philadelphia, and infection set in.

"They figured it went through my bloodstream, and a bug like that finds the weakest point in your body. For some reason, it settled in my left knee," Sherk said.

"He came to the meeting after the Philadelphia game, and his leg swelled so big they couldn't get his pant leg off," Rutigliano said.

Sherk was hospitalized for five weeks. He nearly lost the leg and his life.

"The reason was, I continued to have a fever," he said. "That's a high indication the infection is alive and looking for the next spot. They gave me a really strong antibiotic to fight the infection because they didn't know at first what it was. And I had an allergic reaction to that antibiotic and it kept my temperature up about 100 degrees.

"It was kind of scary. I had the best of care at the Cleveland Clinic. But I can remember waking up and seeing this doctor leaning over my bed one early morning. He probably thought he was doing a good thing, I'm sure, but he looked down on me and said, 'God has put a terrible burden on you.'"

After months of rest followed by strenuous rehabilitation, Sherk recovered the 35 pounds lost and regained his playing weight of 250. He tried to come back in 1981, but the knee wouldn't allow it.

Sherk is philosophical about the opportunities lost because of his injury.

More than 20 years later, he disclosed the emotional pain of not being able to play in the Kardiac Kids season of 1980. He watched most of that Cinderella season unfold from his home

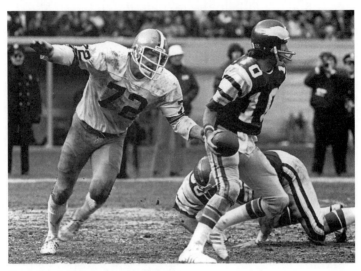

Jerry Sherk (Photo by Paul Tepley)

in southern California, and then joined the team on the sideline for the playoff game against the Oakland Raiders.

Sherk said he had mixed emotions before Brian Sipe's interception throw in the end zone resulted in the 14-12 heartbreaking loss.

"To be truthful, there was a part of me that felt, 'Brian, throw an interception,'" Sherk said of his thoughts before the fateful play. "I didn't want to miss [playing in the Super Bowl]. I so wanted to be on the field."

Sherk and Sipe became closer friends after each retired. They live with their families 10 miles apart in Encinitas, California, 25 miles north of San Diego. After retirement, Sherk stepped easily into a second career as a photographer.

He completed a graduate degree in psychology and now helps organizations develop youth mentoring programs.

Sherk is considered by many to be the best defensive tackle to play for the Browns. He does not brood over the fact his career was cut short by the staph infection.

"I really am just happy to be part of that Browns tradition," he said. "There were times in mid-career I can remember, during TV timeouts between quarters, just walking from one end of the field thinking, 'This is a really neat place to be.' It was an absolutely incredible experience. It wasn't all good, but it was amazing.

"When I was playing, I was really on track, for a while, to make the Hall of Fame. I knew Joe Greene was going to make the Hall of Fame, and I kept thinking, are people going to see me when I'm 60 years old and say, 'That's Mean Joe Greene?'

"I think it's better, in some ways [the way his career turned out]. I can't imagine being the Pittsburgh Steelers and having four championships. I mean, what do you do after that?"

GREG PRUITT

The Browns were slow to realize the enormous offensive weapon they had in Greg Pruitt in the 1970s.

"I had a heckuva time trying to convince them I was big enough to play and for them to develop a team to support me and depend on me," Pruitt said.

Once the Browns got over Pruitt's diminutive size, he became their most electrifying player on offense. Starting in 1975, the 5'9" Pruitt had three successive 1,000-yard rushing seasons and barely missed a fourth. His rushing averages those years were 4.9, 4.8, 4.6 and 5.5.

Greg Pruitt (Photo by Paul Tepley)

"But I think Sam Rutigliano was the first coach that realized all of my abilities—not just running, but receiving, throwing, returns, all of that. Unfortunately, I hurt my knee, so that never really developed."

Pruitt was just entering his prime as an all-purpose back when he tore a knee ligament in a 1979 game in St. Louis. Prior to the injury, "Do It" Pruitt might run, catch or throw on any down. He threw 18 times on halfback option plays, completing eight—six for touchdowns.

"Greg Pruitt was always a step ahead," Rutigliano said. "We were playing Buffalo, we're way ahead, and he's standing next to me with about four minutes to go and I said, 'Why are you standing here?' He says, 'I want to go in the game.'

"He was always thinking about other things. He needed five more yards to get 100 and reach an incentive in his contract."

As the star player on his Oklahoma University teams, Pruitt gravitated to and excelled in the limelight. Coach Barry Switzer once had a T-shirt designed for the lightning-quick Pruitt. On the front in big block letters was the word "Hello." On the back: "Goodbye."

"We were playing USC and they were No. 1 and he was trying to motivate me for the game," Pruitt said. "He gave me the shirt and had the local newspaper take pictures. And then he said, 'Greg, that's a nice-looking shirt, but I want you to know it's hanging in the USC locker room, so it better be 'hello, goodbye' tomorrow.'

"I rushed for 220-some yards."

Early in his NFL career, Pruitt was noted for running away from tacklers in specially designed tearaway jerseys made of soft mesh. The truth is, he hated them.

"When the other team became aware I had a tearaway jersey in crucial situations, guys would just walk up and tear my jersey and the ref would make me leave the game because it was a rules infraction," Pruitt said. "I spent all my time running to and from the sideline changing jerseys. It threw all my concentration off.

"In order for the jersey to be effective, you couldn't wear anything under it, and it wasn't very pleasant in Cleveland in December."

Peter Hadhazy, the Browns' general manager at the time, was a member of the league committee that eventually outlawed the tearaway jersey.

"I told Greg to give me a couple of them for old times' sake, because they're going to be obsolete," Hadhazy said. "I still have two of Greg's jerseys in my closet in New York."

Pruitt was just a shell of his former self during the Browns' Kardiac Kids season of 1980, though he did contribute 50 receptions. He added 65 catches in 1981 before the Browns traded him to the Los Angeles Raiders.

"If I had to do it over again, I wouldn't have traded him. I'd have made him a receiver," Rutigliano said.

Pruitt made the Pro Bowl as a return specialist in 1983 and won a Super Bowl championship ring with the Raiders.

Upon joining the Raiders, he learned something about Mike Davis, the safety who shattered Cleveland's Super Bowl hopes by intercepting Brian Sipe's pass in the end zone in the 1980 playoff game.

"When I first went to the Raiders, the linebackers and defensive backs were practicing against our pass offense in an 8-on-8 drill," Pruitt said. "Mike Davis couldn't catch a pass. I mean, the ball was just beating him up.

"I knew it was him, but I wanted to make sure this was the same guy in 38 degrees below zero that intercepted the ball that beat us. They said it was. I said, 'It just wasn't meant to be, because this guy can't catch.'"

MIKE PRUITT

Mike Pruitt and Greg Pruitt—drafted three years apart—were not related.

"But we were soul brothers," said Greg, the older of the two Browns backs. "I used to ride Mike all the time, use reverse psychology on him. I'd say, 'Mike, you really want to be like me. Just think, if you turn 34 inside out, who is it?'"

Greg wore No. 34; Mike No. 43.

They couldn't have been more different. Greg was the quick little halfback, flashy and brash. Mike was the bigger, slower fullback.

Personality-wise, Mike was "more laid back and conservative," he said.

Mike Pruitt's early career stumbled after getting drafted in the first round from Purdue University.

Under coach Forrest Gregg, Pruitt started only two games in two years and battled fumbling and confidence problems.

"Forrest hated him, he fumbled so much," recalled Peter Hadhazy, the former general manager.

"I think it was a bit unfair because I didn't play a whole lot," Pruitt said of his fumbling reputation. "The little time I did play, I fumbled a few times. But if you don't get any action, you don't know how to protect the ball."

Two things happened to change Mike Pruitt's fortunes. Gregg was replaced by Sam Rutigliano in 1978, and Greg Pruitt suffered a major knee injury in 1979 and never was the same.

"When Sam took over, it was a new life for me," Mike said.

"Mike Pruitt was the greatest project," Rutigliano said. "He was really down when I got there. He had one foot in the grave and the other on the banana peel. And he just became a great player."

After Pruitt stopped fumbling, he rushed for more than 1,000 yards in four of the next five seasons under Rutigliano. In the 1980 Kardiac Kids season, Mike Pruitt led the Browns in rushing and receiving.

He had as much reason as any to be furious with the ending of the 14-12 playoff loss to the Oakland Raiders. Pruitt's 11-yard run had taken the Browns inside the Raiders' 15-yard line in the final minute.

On second and eight from the 13, Pruitt and Cleo Miller lined up in the big backfield set the Browns used to mash out safe yards on the ground.

"I thought it would be another call for me," Pruitt said. "I figured one more play, up the middle or off tackle. It was so cold, everybody was missing tackles. I thought there was a good possibility I could score or get it close to the goal line where it would be just a chip shot for [Don] Cockroft.

"When I heard the call in the huddle, I thought, 'Man, it's too cold to be trying to throw the ball.' You couldn't grip it, your joints were so cold. With the air being so stiff and cold, you couldn't get much velocity on it."

Brian Sipe's pass intended for Ozzie Newsome then was intercepted in the end zone by Raiders safety Mike Davis.

"Lining up in the backfield, I thought, 'I just hope we don't get an interception,'" Pruitt said. "Then I heard the quiet and the crowd just go, 'Ohhhhhhh.' Then I saw Mike Davis jumping up and down. I hated that."

Pruitt stayed in northeast Ohio after his retirement in 1986. He has run car dealerships in Akron and Lima. He sees his former teammates frequently. They don't talk much about the bitter ending of the 1980 playoff game.

"It's a bad memory," he said. "It doesn't come up."

Don Cockroft

Don Cockroft thought he was succeeding Lou Groza when he was made the Browns' surprise third-round draft choice from Adams State (Colorado) in 1967.

He wound up replacing two Browns legends—Groza as placekicker and Gary Collins as punter. Collins, a starting receiver, had doubled as punter for six years.

"I don't think Gary wanted to punt any more," Cockroft said. "Early on in my rookie year, Gary ran one of those 30-yard 'out' routes on third down and came back to the sideline and said, 'Cockroft, get your ass out there and punt the ball.'"

Cockroft did double duty for nine years and continued as the Browns' place-kicker through the 1980 season. He was the second-last of the straight-ahead kickers to retire from the NFL.

Unbeknownst to most, Cockroft played the 1980 season with torn cartilage in his left knee and a herniated disk in his back. His accuracy and confidence suffered.

So Cockroft understood completely when coach Sam Rutigliano disdained a field goal try and called one more offensive play from the 13-yard line in the playoff game against the Oakland Raiders in subzero temperatures and frigid wind chill.

"I had made my last two field goals in the game, but earlier I missed a 45-yarder when the ball was actually slipping on ice and I did miss an extra point down at that [open] end of the stadium," Cockroft said.

"We were moving down there with the wind coming in and I remember telling Brian [Sipe], 'Whatever you do, get it on the right hash mark.' I was right next to Sam on the sideline when he told Brian the play. I heard Sam tell Brian, 'Whatever you do, throw it into Lake Erie.'"

Sipe's pass was intercepted in the end zone, and the Browns lost, 14-12.

Two days after the loss, Cockroft's heart was ripped out when the big news in *The Plain Dealer* carried the headline: "Browns sign kicker Dave Jacobs."

"In other words, who lost the game?" Cockroft said. "I got a call from Art Modell apologizing for that headline the next day. But that hurt a lot. I don't know how to describe it. I knew my career was over right then and there."

Rutigliano cut Cockroft the following summer for Jacobs, a soccer-style specialist who swung a tiny size seven shoe.

"I looked at Sam and said, 'You've heard of flaky kickers? Well, you've got one now,'" Cockroft recalled. "I said if this kid misses some kicks early on, you've got a problem. He went four out of 12 before they got rid of him."

Cockroft retired as the second leading scorer in Browns history behind Groza. He is also the franchise's most prolific punter.

"Don's never forgiven me," Rutigliano said. "Jacobs couldn't kick after I gave him the job. The moment that he won the job, he had a grapefruit in his esophagus."

LYLE ALZADO

Lyle Alzado was a celebrity character on a national scale before he came to the Browns.

One month before the defensive end was acquired from the Denver Broncos for three draft picks in the summer of 1979, Alzado fought the great Muhammad Ali eight rounds in a boxing exhibition in Denver's Mile High Stadium.

Alzado had a penchant for the spotlight, and it sometimes obscured his playing ability. He was the NFL defensive Player of the Year in 1977, the year his Orange Crush defense carried the Broncos to the Super Bowl.

"Alzado was one of the toughest guys that I ever had the opportunity to coach," said Sam Rutigliano. "Weird. But underneath all of it was a genuinely nice man."

Alzado was voted a defensive captain in 1980 and led the Browns with nine sacks.

After that season crashed in a playoff loss to the Oakland Raiders, a rumor circulated that quarterback Brian Sipe defied Rutigliano's call for a run and threw the decisive, heartbreaking interception pass. Alzado was fingered as the source of the rumor.

His teammates were simultaneously awed by his ability and bemused by his rampant mood swings.

"He was a big put-on … a big put-on," said running back Greg Pruitt.

"Although it appeared phony, I don't think there was too much phony about him," said tackle Jerry Sherk. "He was, for lack of a better word, unbalanced.

"He would come in one day and be really nice, and the next day you couldn't talk to him. He just kind of lived in a different world than the rest of us. He could be a terrific guy and he was bright. You can't go on Johnny Carson repeatedly and sort of joust with those type of people and not be on the ball.

"And yet there were other parts of his life in public that were a real failure and tragedy."

After the 1981 season, the Browns traded Alzado to the Los Angeles Raiders. With them, he won a Super Bowl championship ring. He retired in 1984, ending a remarkable 15-year career for the native of Bronx, N.Y., who started out at now-defunct Yankton College in South Dakota.

Alzado was diagnosed with brain cancer in 1991. In a cover story in *Sports Illustrated*, he contended the illness was brought on by a career-long usage of steroids and growth hormones.

In the first-person account of his usage, Alzado said he dispensed steroids to Browns players.

"They'd take them in the privacy of their own homes, and it wasn't talked about much—not in the locker room," Alzado wrote.

Sherk, Alzado's roomate, said he had no idea Alzado was using steroids.

Pruitt said, "There were always rumors about who did what. I didn't know. I guess that was something guys that wanted to be big did. If it had made me tall, maybe I would have taken it, too."

Stricken with brain cancer, Alzado dedicated the rest of his life to educating kids about the dangers of steroids. His crusade didn't last long. He died in 1992—13 months after the diagnosis—at the age of 43.

HENRY BRADLEY

When the Browns lost their best defensive lineman, Jerry Sherk, to a mysterious staph infection in the 10th week of the 1979 season, they called on Henry Bradley to fill in.

Bradley had been cut in August and was making a living in the Cleveland area as a truck driver.

The following season, the Browns switched to a 3-4 defense, and Bradley fit perfectly as the nose tackle in the middle of the line.

"Henry was the most durable, non-quick guy," coach Sam Rutigliano recalled. "In practice, you had to get him out of there because he was going to get somebody hurt. He played full speed all the time."

The Browns went on to have a fanciful season in 1980. The team earned the nickname the Kardiac Kids because they pulled out so many victories with last-minute heroics.

But one time the tables turned on them.

Needing a victory in the 15th game to clinch their first AFC Central championship, the Browns blew a 23-9 lead to the Minnesota Vikings. The Browns were still ahead, 23-22, with four seconds to play.

The Vikings won when Tommy Kramer completed a Hail Mary touchdown pass from 46 yards to Ahmad Rashad.

When that game is recalled, Browns players generally point to what happened next.

As the Browns slinked off the field with chins dragging the turf, the game officials instructed Rutgliano that the Vikings would have to kick the extra point.

"I said, 'Are you kidding me? My guys are devastated. They're off the field,'" Rutigliano recalled.

The coach managed to gather 11 players to line up for the extra point.

Bradley blocked the kick.

JOE (TURKEY) JONES

How did Joe Jones, a defensive end drafted in the second round in 1970, acquire one of the most colorful nicknames in Browns history?

Jones's story was that he was given the nickname Turkey by Tennessee State teammate Claude Humphrey, who invited him to a Thanksgiving Day dinner at Humphrey's farm.

"He said I had a physique like a turkey—long arms and a bulging chest. It stuck," Jones once said.

The moniker became even more appropriate when he joined the Browns.

As a rookie, Jones was a victim of the phantom turkey chase orchestrated by veteran players and coaches. The day before Thanksgiving, rookies were given complicated driving instructions to a farm where they supposedly could pick up free turkeys. Those that had the perseverance to find the farm learned that the free turkey was a hoax.

"They pulled the same joke in his second year, and he went back," said Peter Hadhazy, Browns general manager in the mid-1970s. "He's the only guy in the history of the Browns that went back the second year."

Jones became a locker room legend.

"The best thing I can tell you about him is this," said former coach Sam Rutigliano. "He goes to [equipment manager] Morrie Kono and said he needed a shoelace. Morrie asks, 'Is it right or left?' and Joe says, 'I don't know. I'll go back to my locker and check.'"

"A spaceman in a world of his own," Hadhazy recalled. "Walked to the beat of his own drummer. But always a pleasant guy."

Joe (Turkey) Jones (Photo by Paul Tepley)

He wasn't pleasant on the afternoon of October 10, 1976, however. In a game against the Pittsburgh Steelers, Jones made one of the most violent plays in Browns history. It became a metaphor for the brutality of the Browns-Steelers rivalry.

In the fourth quarter of a game won by the Browns, 18-16, Jones crashed through the Pittsburgh line and grabbed Terry Bradshaw around the waist. He lifted the big Steelers quarterback off his feet and planted him head-first to the ground.

"I thought Turkey had killed him," Browns guard Henry Sheppard said later.

Bradshaw was carried off on a stretcher with a bruised spinal cord. He was flown back to Pittsburgh with his upper body strapped to his seat as a precaution against a broken neck.

"He shouldn't have done it and he realized he shouldn't have done it," Hadhazy said. "I think he was frustrated. The Steelers beat us so often and Bradshaw was so hard to sack because he was so strong and mobile."

Jones never publicly apologized for the violent act, but he did talk with Bradshaw after the game.

"Typical Turkey," Hadhazy said over 25 years later. "He had no reaction one way or the other. He wasn't happy, wasn't remorseful.

"I don't think he even got fined for that play. Nowadays, that would merit a suspension."

DINO HALL

At 5'7" and 165 pounds, Dino Hall was the smallest player with the Browns from 1979 through '83. He carried that distinction with him on every team he ever played, including peewee football at age seven. Boy, did he hate it, too.

"Dino Hall wanted to fight me one day," said tackle Doug Dieken. "I gave him a ride to practice one day. In the car, all he talked about was why the coaches wouldn't play him other than as a third-down back. I said, 'They're afraid you couldn't pick up the linebacker on a blitz.' He was really pissed."

Hall came to the Browns as the Division III national rushing champion from Glasboro State in New Jersey. The Browns signed him as an undrafted free agent at the urging of Denny Lynch, the team's director of operations, an alum of Glasboro State.

"He was a great little athlete, so we brought him in and I cut him," said Sam Rutigliano. "Dino said, 'You're making a big mistake, Coach.' And he was right. He ended up playing for five years."

Hall was re-signed when kick returner Keith Wright was lost with a knee injury in the fifth game.

In Hall's first pro game, he tied an NFL record with nine kickoff returns for 172 yards against Pittsburgh. He still holds Browns career records for kick returns and yards.

Hall carried the ball only 27 times at his natural position of running back, but he made the most of them, averaging 7.2 yards an attempt.

"We played St. Louis his rookie year and put him in at the end of the game to knock the clock down, and he ran 52 yards for a touchdown," Rutigliano said. "He was a tremendously determined guy with unbelievable self-confidence. And he had no fear."

THOM DARDEN

By the time the Browns' magical season of 1980 unfolded, safety Thom Darden was in his eighth year and winding down his career.

The first-round selection from Michigan in 1972 peaked in 1978 with 10 interceptions. He surpassed Warren Lahr as the franchise's all-time ball hawk. Now he was being described as savvy rather than quick.

But he would be the central character in two of the most memorable plays of the unforgettable Kardiac Kids season.

In the 15th game against Minnesota, the Browns had a chance to clinch their first division championship. The Vikings were embroiled in their own torrid division race and needed a win to avoid elimination.

On an unseasonably mild December afternoon in Bloomington, Minnesota, the Browns blew a 23-9 lead in the fourth quarter. They lost, 28-23, when Tommy Kramer completed a desperation Hail Mary pass of 46 yards to Ahmad Rashad as time expired.

On the play, Darden and Ron Bolton both batted the ball trying to break up the pass. The ball deflected to Rashad in the end zone.

"If I could have crawled underneath the ground, I would have," Darden said 23 years later. "It was my responsibility to either intercept the ball or knock it down. I had it in my hands. I didn't do what I was supposed to do, and I just wanted to crawl into the ground in Metropolitan Stadium."

The Browns traveled to rival Cincinnati the next week for another chance at winning the AFC Central Division.

On the Bengals' first offensive possession, Darden made the play that unfairly defined his career. He read a formation the Browns had practiced for all week and knocked Cincinnati receiver Pat McInally unconscious leaping for a pass.

"It was a high throw, we both went up and I tried to hit him in the chest," Darden said. "My first hit was in the chest, and then it raised up to his neck. He went backwards from the head and swallowed his tongue. They had to grab his tongue and pull it out. That was rather scary."

The Browns were penalized 15 yards for the hit and McInally was taken off the field on a stretcher. But he returned in the second quarter.

"He came back and caught a touchdown pass, so obviously I didn't hit him hard enough," Darden said.

The Browns prevailed, 27-24, to end the Pittsburgh Steelers' rule of the AFC Central.

Darden later was fined $1,000 by the league office. He spent one more season in the league, labeled as a dirty player.

Darden intercepted three more balls in his last year to extend his franchise record to 45. His season record of 10 lasted 23 years until Anthony Henry matched it in 2001.

"Today, it doesn't seem that guys are ball hawks like the old days," Darden said. "They're more concerned about making the great hits. I always considered myself a ball hawker."

CHAPTER 4

The 1980s

BILL COWHER

Nothing foretold coaching greatness in Bill Cowher's playing career. He was a backup linebacker and special teams player for three seasons beginning in 1980.

But former teammate Doug Dieken recalled a golf match with Cowher that demonstrated an uncanny competitiveness.

"He hit a ball that landed on the roof of a shanty near a green," Dieken remembered. "It wasn't out of bounds, so rather than take a penalty and play the ball after a drop, he climbed up on the roof and played it from there. Then he lost his footing on the way down and fell."

Cowher turned out to be a much better coach than a player or a golfer.

Upon retirement from the Philadelphia Eagles, Cowher rejoined the Browns as special teams coach under Marty Schottenheimer in 1985. At 28, Cowher was the second youngest assistant coach in the NFL at the time.

As special teams coach, Cowher quickly earned a reputation as a sideline maniac who would bang into everything and anybody in his way as he followed the action of a kickoff from the bench area.

He was elevated to secondary coach in 1987. After the following season ended in a heartbreaking playoff loss, Schottenheimer was fired and his staff fanned out to find new opportunities.

Commiserating with other unemployed assistants at the unofficial coaches convention in Mobile, Alabama, in December of 1988, Cowher vowed, "I'm going to be a head coach in this league some day."

Cowher followed Schottenheimer to Kansas City as his defensive coordinator for three seasons. In early 1991, he was interviewed by the Browns for their vacant head coach job, but he was considered too young and "too much like Marty."

The next year, Cowher got his break. He was hired by his hometown Pittsburgh Steelers to replace the legendary Chuck Noll. He was 34.

In four years, Cowher became the youngest coach to lead his team to the Super Bowl. He would take the Steelers to the playoffs in each of his first six seasons, matching Paul Brown as the only head coach to do so.

By 2003, Cowher was in his 12th season as Steelers head coach, making him the longest-tenured coach in the league. He forged a 14-4 record against the Browns, including victories in the only two postseason meetings of the longtime rivals.

When the Browns went on hiatus following the 1995 season, Cowher was presented with a chair from old Cleveland Municipal Stadium and a bronzed hook from the relic's ancient locker room to commemorate his time in Cleveland.

He wasn't a gracious visitor when the expansion team was born in 1999. The NFL selected the Steelers to christen new

Cleveland Browns Stadium, and Cowher inspired his team to a 43-0 mashing of the new Browns in a nationally televised game.

"I guess I look at Cleveland as a place that will always be a part of my life," Cowher said. "Every time I think of Cleveland, I think of Doug Dieken, Robert Jackson and the Kardiac Kids of 1980.

"I remember whenever we went to Pittsburgh as a player, Clay Matthews and Dick Ambrose would always want to come to my house and have my mom make dinner so they could keep their meal money. Those guys were happy to get a free meal."

JOE DELAMIELLEURE

Joe DeLamielleure clutched a rosary in his pocket. On a chain around his thick neck he wore two medals, one of Saint Joseph and one of Saint Sebastian.

This was on the eve of the biggest day of Joe D.'s life after football. He was a finalist for the Pro Football Hall of Fame. The selection meeting was less than 24 hours away, and Joe D. relied on his Catholic faith to get him through the agonizing wait.

"My whole life I've worn the medal of Saint Joseph, patron saint of families," he said. "I'm one of 10 kids in my family. My wife is one of eight. We have five of our own, and we adopted two Korean boys.

"Saint Sebastian, they shot him with arrows and he wouldn't die. They had to find another means to kill him. They beat him. He was indestructible and became known as the patron saint of athletes."

DeLamielleure credits Saint Sebastian for looking out for him. In 13 NFL seasons, eight with Buffalo and five with the Browns, DeLamielleure never missed a game because of injury.

A squatty 6'3" and 254 pounds, Joe D. was naturally strong and athletic. He won the AFC arm-wrestling competition one off season, and the NFL racquetball tournament another time.

"Athletically, I don't think a lot of guards could do what I did," he said.

His reputation was made in Buffalo, where he helped make O.J. Simpson a football legend. DeLamielleure was a key member of the Juice's "Electric Company," the nickname given Buffalo's run-blocking offensive line in the 1970s.

In DeLamielleure's first season in Buffalo, Simpson rushed for an NFL-record 2,003 yards in 14 games. In 1976, Simpson set another record with 273 yards in one game. At the time, the collegiate record of 375 was held by Eric Allen of Michigan State. DeLamielleure blocked for him, too.

Joe D.'s relationship with the Bills broke down in a contract dispute with Buffalo coach Chuck Knox. Figuring he had seen his better days, Knox traded him to Cleveland for two future second-round draft choices.

"We needed to protect [quarterback] Brian Sipe," Browns coach Sam Rutigliano said.

DeLamielleure made a smooth transition from a running offense to a passing offense. Sipe set Browns passing records and won the league MVP award. Joe D. was elected to the Pro Bowl for the sixth straight year.

Mike Giddings, an independent scout employed by several NFL teams, rated DeLamielleure among the best linemen of his time.

"He was one of the best at what I call short-set pass protecting," Giddings said. "You couldn't bull-rush him, couldn't stuff him. He would stick out those hands and no one would get by him."

DeLamielleure played in Cleveland through the 1984 season, then returned to Buffalo to retire with the Bills in 1985. In 1991, he unretired at the age of 40 to play arena football in Charlotte, North Carolina.

He was superstitious to the end.

"I used to put fruit in my socks against my skin," he said. "I met a guy a long time ago who was a doctor for the king of Saudi Arabia. He showed me that holding fruit or vegetables to your body made you stronger.

"I got to putting apple slices in my socks. I never got hurt, so I kept doing it. I was playing arena football and twisted my ankle. The trainer runs over and cuts my sock to look at my ankle and four apple slices spilled out.

"He looked at me, surprised, and I said, 'You never know when you're going to get hungry.'"

On January 25, 2003, DeLamielleure's faith was rewarded. Beating long odds, he was elected to the Hall of Fame. He figured the time was right.

"This was my 13th time up for the Hall of Fame," he said. "I signed my first contract on Friday the 13th when I was drafted. There are 13 letters in my last name. I played 13 years in the NFL. O.J. rushed for 2003 and it's the Class of 2003."

And one other thing.

"A friend of mine noticed that the news that I made the Hall of Fame came across the Associated Press wire at 3:13 p.m., EST."

PAUL MCDONALD

In sunny southern California, Paul McDonald quarterbacked the USC Trojans to two Rose Bowl victories and one national championship.

But in cold, gray Cleveland, McDonald's career never thawed.

He was drafted in the fourth round in 1980 to eventually succeed Brian Sipe. The left-handed McDonald could throw a pretty spiral in practice. On Sundays, McDonald froze.

That was literally the case in the 1980 season playoff game against the Oakland Raiders.

The week before the game, coach Sam Rutigliano resisted the urge to replace the rookie McDonald with Sipe as holder on Don Cockroft's placekicks.

"McDonald was in another world, he was so cold," Rutigliano remembered.

You could tell immediately that McDonald was spooked by the subzero temperatures in Cleveland Municipal Stadium that January 4 afternoon.

"He came out in rubber scuba gloves," guard Joe DeLamielleure said.

In the epic game won by Oakland, 14-12, Cockroft missed two field goals and had one extra point blocked. Another field goal try was aborted when McDonald fumbled the snap.

"That was probably one of the reasons [McDonald] didn't make it [as a starting quarterback]," Rutigliano said. "He just didn't have what Sipe had."

Rutigliano chose to hand the job over to McDonald ahead of Sipe after the 1983 season. Sipe, 34, signed with the fledgling United States Football League.

Rutigliano was fired after McDonald went 1-7 as the starter.

"We just misevaluated McDonald," Rutigliano said. "If I had been smarter and kept Brian, we might have won eight or nine games and I would have survived."

CLEVELAND CROSBY

The last line of the Browns' official biography of 1980 second-round draft choice Cleveland Crosby of Arizona read, "Believe it or not, his middle name is Pittsburgh."

Well, believe it or not, one day Crosby showed up in a team meeting room prior to an exhibition game in Minnesota wearing a Pittsburgh Steelers T-shirt.

Veteran players were irate that this rookie would disrespect his own team so badly by wearing the shirt of its chief rival. Coach Sam Rutigliano promptly made Crosby remove the shirt and sit in the meeting bare-chested.

"When he fell out of the tree, he hit every limb on the way down," longtime offensive tackle Doug Dieken said of Crosby. "One time I volunteered to go against him one on one in training camp. It was at the time of that Goodyear commercial. I got down in my stance and said to him, 'Look, the Goodyear blimp.' And he looked up."

Recalled Rutigliano: "The day of the draft, defensive coordinator Marty Schottenheimer said, 'I visited there. We don't want him.' Director of player personnel Tommy Prothro and I had a major, major discussion on him. We didn't want him and we ended up taking him, and Marty was absolutely right."

Crosby, hailed "as good as anyone in the draft" for his pure athletic ability by a Bowns scout, was released after two regular-season games.

CHARLES WHITE

In 1980, the Browns used their first draft choice for the first time on a reigning Heisman Trophy winner—running back Charles White of University of Southern California.

It seemed like a good match. The Browns had not had a league rushing champion since Leroy Kelly in 1967. And White had outgained such USC luminaries as O.J. Simpson and Mike Garrett with a university-record 5,598 yards in four seasons— the second highest figure in an NCAA career at the time.

But it was not to be.

"Charles White was a mistake," said Sam Rutigliano, the Browns coach who created one of the league's highest-scoring offenses. "Charles White was an I-formation running back, a banger, a tough guy. We needed more guys like Calvin Hill and Greg Pruitt. He wasn't very quarterback-friendly. He didn't have very good hands."

White had rushing totals of 279 and 342 yards in his first two seasons. At USC, those were typical games for him. It was after his second season of 1981 that Rutigliano became aware that White had a drug problem.

By then, Rutigliano had started the revolutionary self-help program he called the Inner Circle. It was based on voluntary enlistment protected by confidentiality. One day, a player being treated in the program told Rutigliano that White needed help.

"He said, 'Coach, I know you said there would be anonymity, but if you don't call Charlie White in, he's gonna die. I'm worried about the direction he's going,'" Rutigliano recalled.

"That was the beginning of the confrontation, to me. I flew Charlie in from L.A. and sat him down and said, 'It's 10:51.

You either do what I tell you by 11 o'clock or I'll put you on waivers and you're finished. And I'll yell and I'll tell.'

"So I arranged for him to see that moment Dr. Glenn Collins, who was in charge of the program. I told him I loved him and would help him and [wife] Judy save his life. Subsequently, he went with John Robinson and I think he's got his life straightened out now."

White publicly acknowledged treatment for a drug problem during the 1982 training camp. He became the only player in the Inner Circle to publicly identify himself.

White rejoined Robinson, his college coach, with the Los Angeles Rams after the Browns waived him in 1985. In 1987, the Rams traded future Hall of Famer Eric Dickerson. White took over and led the NFL in rushing with 1,374 yards and 11 touchdowns.

White did have other relapses—a drug-related arrest in 1987 and an NFL suspension in 1988 for drinking. He eventually returned to USC as a special assistant and assistant coach for Robinson at his alma mater.

The day of his appointment, Robinson said, "Charlie was the toughest, most intense running back I ever coached."

OZZIE NEWSOME

You can make the case that Ozzie Newsome's big butt got him into the Hall of Fame.

Before the Browns made him the second of two first-round choices in 1978, coach Sam Rutigliano sent receivers coach Rich Kotite to Birmingham, Alabama, to inspect Newsome's butt. Newsome was an All-America receiver for Coach Paul (Bear) Bryant at Alabama.

Ozzie Newsome (Photo by Paul Tepley)

"I said to Rich, 'Just find out if he's got a big ass,'" Rutigliano said.

Newsome was 6'2" and 235 pounds when he reported to the Browns' first team minicamp as a rookie. He lined up at receiver the whole time.

After the minicamp, Rutigliano told him, "You've proven to us you can be a good receiver. We think you can be a great tight end."

Rutigliano hit the bull's-eye with that call. He was the perfect coach to exploit Newsome in defensive mismatches and develop him into a Hall of Fame tight end.

"Ozzie was like hitting the inside straight for us," Rutigliano said. "In those days, every [defense] was in a double zone. Ozzie changed that, because he went right to the middle of the defense. Then we came up with the slot formation and split him out, and they put a safety on him."

Newsome said: "In those days, you had those strong safeties with those neck collars, quasi-linebackers, and I'd split out. They were out of their element and I was in my element."

Newsome averaged 15.5 yards per catch his rookie year. He went on to become the most prolific pass-catching tight end in NFL history until his 662 receptions were topped by Shannon Sharpe in 2002. Newsome was the fifth tight end inducted into the Hall of Fame in 1999.

He is one of the few Browns whose careers stretched across three decades—the 1970s, '80s and '90s. Newsome also was the only player to have a central role in the offense during the distinctly different eras of quarterbacks Brian Sipe and Bernie Kosar.

"Both were great leaders and both had that charisma," Newsome said. "Both could make players better around them. Both had great anticipation."

Upon retirement in 1990, Newsome stayed on with the Browns as a special assignment scout and then was made an assistant coach under Bill Belichick. It was in the tumultuous 1993 season, during which Belichick released the popular Kosar, that Newsome made the pivotal decision of his post-playing career.

"The day after the whole Kosar thing transpired, Belichick came in and said, 'I've got to go back to being a head coach. Do you want to run the offense?'" Newsome recalled. "I said no, I really don't want to be a coach.

"That was probably the biggest decision I've made. At that point personnel was the true route I wanted to take. Would I now be the head coach at University of Alabama if I had taken Belichick's offer? Maybe."

Newsome said choosing to stay in personnel was a tougher decision for him than the controversial one he later made in 1996—when he agreed to follow owner Art Modell after he moved his team from Cleveland to Baltimore. Once detached from Cleveland, Modell put Newsome in charge of personnel of his Baltimore Ravens.

"Mr. Modell had been very good to me," Newsome said. "The toughest part was leaving Cleveland, but the job and the opportunity were tailor-made for me."

After some growing pains in Baltimore—during which the cash-strapped franchise was forced to play one season with no practice squad and an overall roster smaller than the rest of the league—Newsome deftly built the Ravens into champions. And when they won the Super Bowl in the 2000 season, Newsome was able to bury the personal ghosts that had haunted him in Cleveland, such as "The Pass" of the 1980 playoffs, "The Drive" of 1986 and "The Fumble" of 1987.

"I guess all the bad luck we had in Cleveland wasn't me, because I've got my Super Bowl ring," Newsome said.

Modell rewarded Newsome by naming him vice president and general manager years later. The promotion made Newsome one of the highest-ranking African-American executives in the NFL.

CLAY MATTHEWS

Long, golden-brown hair and surfer-boy looks belied the work ethic that Clay Matthews brought to the Browns from the campus of University of Southern California in the 1978 college draft.

Although he grew up in a white-collar world—his father Clay Sr. was a CEO for several corporations after a brief NFL career—Matthews was a blue-collar player who bonded easily with football-mad Cleveland in the 1980s.

"Everybody wants to know what's going on with the team in Cleveland," Matthews said in a visit to a Browns reunion seven years after his career ended. "They care about it. In other places, if it's the hot thing to do, it's all right. But here it's always the 'in' thing to do. I liked it here from the beginning."

It became a ritual for Matthews to make the 3,000-mile cross-country drive from his southern California home to Browns training camp in a 1973 Mercury Capri. He drove the Capri long after the odometer stopped working.

As a player, Matthews often was used to plug leaks at any of the team's linebacker positions. When the arrival of the physically gifted Chip Banks moved Matthews from the more glam-

Clay Matthews (© Brockway Sports Photos)

orous pass-rushing role, Matthews did not pout. He made the Pro Bowl playing the other side.

"When I came to the Browns, he and Chip Banks were at the top of their game, and Clay was the best player in the NFL," said quarterback Gary Danielson.

Matthews was "real different off the field," Danielson added.

Matthews earned a business degree with honors and eventually an MBA. He used words like "stimuli" in media interviews. He solved the *New York Times* crossword puzzle each day—in pen.

If he was not stimulated enough by the game plan, boredom would overtake Matthews.

"Sometimes I wish that I could go over to the coaches' office on Monday or Tuesday and work with them on the game plan so I can do the things that I think are really exciting," he said in an interview in early 1987. "I'll just sit and think of ways to make unusual plays. I think about lateraling the ball. I envision these unusual scenarios."

The comments were prophetic. In a game against Cincinnati the next season, Matthews intercepted a pass, ran for 36 yards, and then lateraled the ball to defensive end Carl (Big Daddy) Hairston, who added 40 yards to the play.

But Matthews's most famous lateral didn't turn out as well. In a 1989 game in Houston with the playoffs on the line, Matthews picked up a fumble and tossed a lateral in the vicinity of defensive lineman Chris Pike. The 6'8", 300-pound Pike reacted to the ball as if it were a live grenade.

Houston recovered the loose ball and scored on its next play to take the lead. The Browns pulled out a 24-20 win with a late touchdown to earn the division championship, removing the goat horns from Matthews.

"If we'd have lost, I would have put Clay on the propeller for the plane ride back to Cleveland," coach Bud Carson said.

"That's the most ridiculous play I remember in my career," recalled Ernie Accorsi, the director of football operations, 15 years later.

Matthews wore a T-shirt at practice the next week that said, "No Brains. No Headache."

"I don't have a headache and some people are making the case that I don't have any brains," he said. "I guess the smart thing to do would have been to fall down."

In truth, Matthews was singed by the criticism he received for the play.

Remembered Dave Puzzuoli, one of Matthews's best friends on the team: "It kind of hurt him. He would say, 'They don't realize how hard I train, how hard I work and what I've done for the team. OK, I screwed up. But I'm trying to make something happen.'"

The following week, Matthews sealed the Browns' 34-30 playoff victory over Buffalo by intercepting Jim Kelly at the goal line on the last play of the game. He fell to his knees, clutching the ball.

Matthews holds the Browns record with 232 games played. Counting his final three seasons with the Atlanta Falcons, Matthews's 278 games rank third all-time among NFL position players.

His younger brother, Bruce, starred for 19 seasons on the offensive line of the Houston Oilers/Tennessee Titans. They competed against each other twice a season from 1983, Bruce's first year, to 1993.

Clay never made it to the Super Bowl. When Bruce ultimately did with Tennessee in the 1999 season, Clay said, "He's always trying to outdo me."

MARTY SCHOTTENHEIMER

The night after a dismal 12-9 loss in Cincinnati in the middle of the 1984 season, Marty Schottenheimer was summoned to Art Modell's palatial house in Waite Hill, Ohio. The 41-year-old defensive coordinator was offered the job to succeed fired Sam Rutigliano as Browns coach.

"He was a young guy with stars in his eyes and he saw an opportunity," Rutigliano said.

Never a head coach before, Schottenheimer demanded a long-term commitment before accepting the job.

"He was adamant that it wasn't an interim job, because he felt they wouldn't play for him if they thought he wouldn't be back," said Ernie Accorsi, director of football operations. "He wanted a fairly long-term commitment, and Art gave it to him."

The move paid off. Schottenheimer steered the 1-7 team to a 4-4 finish and then embarked on a playoff run not seen since the Paul Brown days.

The Browns won the AFC Central Division three years in a row and made the playoffs a fourth consecutive season as a wild card.

"My first training camp in 1985 I told the squad our objective was to win the championship, to win it now," Schottenheimer recalled almost 20 years later. "They said people would think I was smoking something, but that's the way I believe it.

"I recall at the end of the year I met with Ozzie Newsome and Ozzie said, 'You know, Coach, at the outset I want to tell you something. I thought you were smoking something talking that way.'"

The Browns got close to the Super Bowl two times under Schottenheimer, but they were repelled each time by John Elway and the Denver Broncos.

It was on Schottenheimer's watch that the Browns suffered two of their most excruciating playoff losses in the 1986 and '87 season AFC championship games—the first was dubbed "the Drive" of Denver's John Elway and the second was "the Fumble" of Earnest Byner.

"The only one I ever reflect on is 'the Drive' because we had every opportunity in the world to win that football game," Schottenheimer said in 2001. "In that particular game, I can virtually recite 'the Drive.' That has bothered me."

Bookish with wire-rimmed eyeglasses, stuffily conservative and stubborn to a fault, Schottenheimer became known for corny phrases and a habit of breaking into tears in speeches to his team.

"He was real emotional. He used to get pretty worked up," said defensive tackle Dave Puzzuoli.

"We used to bet on when he'd cry," Newsome said.

A lasting image of Schottenheimer was captured on the team's highlight film one season. Players were huddled around him at the start of a playoff game, and Schottenheimer exhorted, "There's a gleam, men. Let's get the gleam."

"He was a little bit sappy to some guys," said quarterback Gary Danielson. "But I enjoyed playing for him. I really did."

Newsome said Schotteneheimer earned instant respect.

"The first game he coached we played New Orleans, and he instituted something I think we all hated," Newsome said. "He made us all watch every game together on Mondays. Offense, defense, everyone. It brought about accountability."

Schottenheimer's best coaching job may have been in what proved to be his last season in 1988. That year, the Browns made the playoffs as a wild card despite suffering five injuries to quarterbacks.

But after the season ended in a one-point loss to Houston in the playoffs, Modell requested Schottenheimer postpone a vacation to Florida with his family and meet him on December 26.

"Art said he'd pay the expenses," Accorsi recalled. "I blame myself, to a point. I should have figured out a way to get Marty to Florida."

In the meeting, Modell wanted Schottenheimer to replace himself as offensive coordinator and reassign his brother, Kurt, who was special teams coach. Schottenheimer resisted.

"I remember this very vividly," Accorsi said. "Nothing was really resolved in the meeting. Marty left the meeting, drove to his office, and somebody showed him the story in *The Plain Dealer.*"

Under the headline "Modell won't let coaches stand pat," Modell publicly outlined the steps he planned to take before he introduced them to Schottenheimer.

"Marty called me and said, 'It's over,'" Accorsi remembered. "That was the last straw. We all wanted him to stay. I thought he'd done his best coaching job."

Schottenheimer felt he could find another job with no problem. He did.

He wound up coaching for the Kansas City Chiefs for 10 years, and then the Washington Redskins and San Diego Chargers, too. He was the first man in the modern-day NFL to coach four different teams.

TOM COUSINEAU

Sam Rutigliano says Tom Cousineau "probably got the worst deal of any real outstanding player that I've ever been around."

One of the most highly recruited players ever from St. Edward High School in Cleveland, Cousineau went on to gain

All-America honors as a linebacker at Ohio State under Woody Hayes.

Playing for the hometown Browns was never on his radar screen, however. And almost 20 years later, he described his four years in Cleveland as "torture."

"I was just a miserable human being," he said.

Cousineau was the NFL's first overall draft choice in 1979. But contract negotiations with the Buffalo Bills bogged down, and Cousineau signed a five-year deal with the Montreal Alouettes of the Canadian Football League.

After three years, Cousineau had the option to leave for the NFL. His stock was still high enough to attract a staggering $3.5 million contract from the Houston Oilers. Buffalo had the right to match the offer, and they shocked Cousineau by doing that.

He was further stunned when Browns owner Art Modell traded three draft picks, including his team's No. 1 in 1983, for Cousineau.

"We were never consulted," Cousineau said. "I was trying to get to a 4-3 [defensive system] as a middle linebacker because of my size. The Browns [who played a 3-4 alignment] were one of the teams that we thought wasn't a good fit."

Modell liked the public relations value of acquiring a big-name local star. Rutigliano favored the move on the recommendation of assistant coach Joe Scannella, who was Cousineau's head coach in Montreal.

"The only guy that didn't think it was a good thing—and he really was the most important—was Marty Schottenheimer," Cousineau said.

Schottenheimer was Rutigliano's defensive coordinator.

"The reason I didn't want to be in that [3-4] defense was I wasn't big enough," Cousineau said. "I played at 210 to 212 pounds. That's a really tough mismatch going against offensive guards. You can play inside at that weight if you're covered up by a good defensive front four. Houston had that."

Cousineau ranked in the top three in tackles on the team in three of his four years. But he was nowhere near the player he might have been in a 4-3. His huge contract—highest on the team—caused chemistry problems with other players. The distractions of playing at home didn't help, either.

But the source of Cousineau's misery, he said, was Schottenheimer, who took over for Rutigliano as head coach in the middle of the 1984 season.

"In four years, we barely had a speaking relationship," Cousineau said. "I bet I never exchanged more than half a dozen words with Marty at one time in four years.

"It was misery for me to go to work every day. Marty just made my life pathetically miserable, professionally. He was very antagonistic."

In 1979, the NFL had no free agency as it does today. So Cousineau's decision to spurn the Bills for the CFL was a radical move. His professional growth was stunted in three years in the CFL. The fact he sacrificed those years and still did not have complete freedom to choose his NFL destination afterwards was, in his words, a "serious miscalculation."

"I ended up drinking my own Kool-Aid," he said.

Cousineau was released by Schottenheimer in the 1986 training camp. He joined the San Francisco 49ers and retired the following year.

A few years ago, Cousineau had the occasion to confront Schottenheimer in a chance meeting at Fairlawn Country Club in Akron. Cousineau was driving his daughter to swimming practice when he noticed Schottenheimer on the ninth green near the club's entranceway.

"I said to my daughter, 'Honey, I want you to meet Daddy's old boss,' and pulled the truck over and waited for him to putt out," Cousineau said. "At the right time, I walked to the green, stuck out my hand and said, 'How are you, Marty?'

"I thought he was going to crap his pants. He just stood there, incredulous. He couldn't speak."

Cousineau enjoyed the moment immensely.

EDDIE JOHNSON

Sometimes the players who don't run the fastest, don't weigh the heaviest and don't bench-press the most turn out to be invaluable teammates in ways that can't be measured. One such player was Eddie Johnson.

The linebacker from the University of Louisville came to the Browns in the seventh round of the draft in 1981. He always was counted out in training camp, yet he always won the fight for a roster spot and usually a place in the starting lineup.

Johnson was an inspiration to teammates because of his indefatigable will to survive. He relished the nickname "the Assassin." It aptly described his fearlessness on the field. Later, teammates affectionately called him "Bullet Head," for the way he used his pointed head to tackle.

In the mid-1980s, cornerbacks Hanford Dixon and Frank Minnifield popularized the nickname "dawgs" for members of the defense. Teammates say Johnson was the first to use the expression.

"Instead of saying you were good, he'd say you were a dawg," said nose tackle Dave Puzzuoli. "After a while, he'd just bark to recognize you were playing tough. That was a compliment. Eddie grew up in Georgia, so it was an imitation of the Georgia Bulldogs."

Off the field, Johnson was tireless in giving his time to charitable causes. He became more popular in the Cleveland community after his 10-year career ended in 1990.

"He never turned me down for a community appearance," said Dino Lucarelli, the Browns' alumni director.

Two stories:

From Earnest Byner, a running back who joined the Browns in 1984:

"My first camp, we were having short-yardage and goal-line situations. Gary [Danielson] tossed the ball to me and I started to go to the outside and decided to go downhill full speed. Whap! That's what you heard. I didn't move and the person in front of me didn't move. It was Eddie. I remember looking into his eyes. Those glazing, big, white, intense, beautiful eyes. That's when the respect started."

From Mike Johnson, who started alongside Eddie at inside linebacker:

"Eddie was real tight with a couple pro wrestlers. It was freezing cold and one of them gave him his mask. I remember thinking, 'He's going to wear that mask during the game? Is that even legal?' They were all uptight about our socks and everything. He wore it through the entire game on national television. I remember the steam coming off his breath and him looking like a pro wrestler."

Those stories were told at a memorial for Johnson. He died on January 21, 2003 after a three-year battle with colon cancer. He was 43 and left three teenage children.

Johnson was an inspiration to others right up until the end.

Months before his death, he said of his battle: "I guess when you put things in perspective, you realize you've been blessed in a lot of ways. I've helped a lot of people along the way. I'm at peace with where I'm at. I'm certainly not angry at anyone. I feel I can beat this and whatever it takes to get through it. I've been a fighter all my life. People have always said I can't do things."

When he passed away, former teammates Hanford Dixon, Herman Fontenot, Reggie Langhorne and Felix Wright were at his bedside.

"I was really moved and touched when I heard that," said Ernie Accorsi, the architect of the Browns' playoff teams in the late 1980s. "To me, that just explained what those teams were all about."

BOB GOLIC

Christmas was a festive occasion in the Browns' locker room in the 1980s thanks to nose tackle Bob Golic.

The jovial Golic would put his teammates in the Christmas spirit by decorating his locker each December. The tradition began while Golic was with the New England Patriots. When he joined the Browns in 1982, Golic took it up a few notches.

"I was always a big Christmas guy," Golic said. "I'd put up a couple things, maybe some garland, and guys would make some comments. When I'd catch grief, I'd do it more."

Eventually, left tackle Doug Dieken joined Golic in a competition for the best-decorated locker. Each year, Golic would go to extreme measures to better Dieken's display.

"Dieken would come in with the tacky, redneck display," Golic said. "He had an awful-looking stuffed Santa Claus and a fake tree with players' faces pasted on bulbs. He'd play 'Gramma Got Run Over by a Reindeer' on his sound system.

"I was more into the traditional Christmas decorations. On my top shelf, I'd have a nativity scene with a spotlight shining on the Three Wise Men. I always wanted Matt Bahr up there as my angel. I'd play traditional Christmas carols. I had a real tree. At the end, I actually built a platform from the top of my locker suspended to the ceiling and put up an electric train.

"That's when Clay Matthews, whose locker was next to mine, started complaining about liability and threatened to sue. Somebody would always sabotage my train. It was a lot of fun."

Golic had to make a position change when he joined the Browns. He moved from the glamorous linebacker position to nose tackle, which Golic often likened to a fire hydrant.

"When the Patriots cut me, Bill Davis [personnel director] made the comment, 'Golic used to wrestle in high school and college. It's the same thing—balance, leverage, man against man.' Yeah, he failed to tell me about all the 2-on-1s and 3-on-1s.

"Once I got inside, it did feel like wrestling to me. There was that mano-a-mano aspect. There was a lot of satisfaction right away."

Golic immensely loved playing for his hometown team even though he suffered through two of the AFC championship game losses to Denver. He enjoyed the responsibility of talking to the media. Some teammates accused him of playing up to the media too much, but his personality and willingness to showcase it eventually paid off.

Golic ended his career with the Los Angeles Raiders. His postgame interviews caught the ear of television scouts in Hollywood. Soon after his playing days ended, Golic received bit parts in *Coach*, and other situation comedies. He won a regular role in *Saved by the Bell—the College Years*, a series that lived one season in prime time.

"It wasn't like I was trying [to be an actor]," Golic said. "I just did it as long as it was there. After *Saved by the Bell* got canceled, I found out I missed sports. So I started calling people to try and get back into stuff."

He landed a stint as a football analyst on NBC and later on Fox. Golic now does a sports talk show on radio in Los Angeles.

AL GROSS

In the spring of 1986, NFL owners voted to allow the use of instant replay to help officials make difficult calls. It took exactly three plays into the 1986 season for the replay process to be used.

The Browns opened the '86 season in Chicago against the defending-champion Bears. On the third play from scrimmage, Bears quarterback Jim McMahon was looking the other way when center Jay Hilgenberg's shotgun snap whistled past him.

The ball bounced wildly for 28 yards into the Bears' end zone. Safety Al Gross chased down the ball and snatched it just as he slid out of the end zone. Gross became the first subject of NFL instant replay review.

After a delay of few minutes, replays confirmed that Gross secured possession before his body crossed the end line of the end zone. He was credited with a touchdown.

Gross suffered a knee injury in the second half of the game. He missed the next nine games. Gross was never the same player and was cut after the 1987 season.

CHIP BANKS

Chip Banks ranks high on the list of Browns players who fell short of expectations. That's saying a lot, considering he made the Pro Bowl at outside linebacker in three of his first four seasons in the 1980s.

"Chip Banks, to me, could have been one of the great linebackers to play the game," said his first coach, Sam Rutigliano. "He was a troubled guy. He had flashes of brilliance. If you took Chip Banks and Lawrence Taylor, Chip Banks was better. But you couldn't put inside of him what Lawrence Taylor had."

Banks awed teammates as a physical specimen. He was 6'4" and 245 pounds with a 28-inch waist and ran as fast as safeties. He rarely lifted weights.

"He was the greatest linebacker in the history of Frank Minnifield's football career," said cornerback Frank Minnifield. "It was unbelievable what people did not try to do on his side of the defense.

"When I played the left side with Chip Banks in front of me, people didn't throw slant routes at me. They were afraid Chip would bat them down. Plus, quarterbacks thought he was always too close to them. I recognized that right away, that he made my job easier."

Rutigliano remembers a game against Cincinnati in which Banks stopped in the middle of a pass rush, jumped in the air and intercepted a Ken Anderson pass at the line of scrimmage.

"I've never seen anybody do that," Rutigliano said.

Banks suffered when Marty Schottenheimer succeeded Rutigliano as coach. Schottenheimer did not like the fact that Banks did not participate in the team's fledgling off-season program. Schottenheimer made Clay Matthews the feature linebacker in the pass rush.

"I thought the guy who could've put us over the top that we didn't utilize was Chip," said Ernie Accorsi, director of football operations at the time. "I can still see Chip trotting off the field on the nickel [defense] and the crowd would boo.

"I just thought Chip Banks wasn't that far away from Lawrence Taylor in pure talent. We played him at strong- side linebacker and never rushed him. It affected Chip's pride."

Banks brooded over his reduced role and distanced himself from teammates.

"Not a whole lot of people got along with Chip," Minnifield said. "Chip was a loner and just happened to be a great football player."

Rutigliano said Banks achieved "60 or 70 percent" of his potential. Minnifield agreed that he could have accomplished more.

On draft day in 1987, Schottenheimer shocked his players and their fans by trading Banks to the San Diego Chargers for the No. 5 pick in the draft. He used it to select unheralded Duke linebacker Mike Junkin.

Years later, Banks gained revenge on his former team. Then with the Indianapolis Colts, an inspired Banks recorded four sacks of Bernie Kosar and intercepted one of his passes in a 14-3 defeat of the Browns.

It was the kind of game the Browns always expected out of Banks.

MIKE JUNKIN

On the morning of the 1987 draft, the Browns traded four-time Pro Bowl linebacker Chip Banks and their first-round pick to San Diego for the fifth overall spot in the first round. It was a stunner.

Then came an aftershock—they used the pick to select an unknown linebacker from Duke University named Mike Junkin.

Coach Marty Schottenheimer hyped the selection by disclosing that when area scout Dom Anile first scouted Junkin, he reported that he'd just seen "a mad dog in a meat market."

Years later, Anile moaned, "That will be the epitaph on my tombstone."

Junkin turned out to be one of the Browns' all-time draft busts. Anile was not surprised.

"I wrote him up as a down-the-line first-round, early second-round kind of guy because of production and intelligence," Anile said. "My concerns with Junkin at the time were speed and athletic ability. He was not very fast and not very athletic.

"Mike further produced question marks because he was a 189-pound tight end out of high school and [as a senior at Duke] was a 240-pound linebacker. The concerns were this guy is always going to be hurt or suspended."

Anile said that Schottenheimer's love of Junkin overrided the best advice from his scouts. They preferred taking Penn State's Shane Conlan, who carried a higher grade on the team's draft board.

"All the scouts are in the draft room and there's a major meeting going on in Art Modell's office," Anile recalled. "Art's in there with his 'committee' for quite a while. Finally, Marty comes into the draft room and calls everybody to attention and announces we've just made a trade with San Diego for Chip Banks, and says with the fifth pick in the draft we're taking 'the mad dog in the meat market.'

"And everybody in the room, their jaws dropped. He certainly wasn't the fifth pick in the draft by anybody's estimation."

Compounding the error, Schottenheimer intended to move Junkin to outside linebacker to fill Banks's vacated spot—again defying Anile's best advice.

Junkin's first training camp was interrupted by a 16-day holdout before the Browns signed him to a contract that made him their highest-paid linebacker. His rookie season was a dismal failure, exacerbated by a four-week players' strike and a wrist injury that required eight hours of surgery.

After Schottenheimer was forced out in 1988 and became coach of the Kansas City Chiefs, he took Junkin off the Browns' hands for a late draft choice.

Junkin's one moment of glory came in Milwaukee in the fourth exhibition game of his rookie year. He intercepted a Green Bay pass in overtime and returned it 21 yards for a touchdown to end the droning evening.

It turned out to be a mistaken play.

"He was in the wrong place covering the wrong guy," Schottenheimer said.

EARNEST BYNER

In the 1984 draft, the Browns used their last available choice in the 10th round on an obscure running back from East Carolina named Earnest Byner. No one could have expected this player ultimately to define the highest highs and the lowest lows of the Browns in the late 1980s.

Byner did his job with an almost maniacal focus. Among his quirks was an insistence on running to the end zone on simple handoffs in practice.

"The work ethic that guy had was incredible," said Kevin Mack, who joined Byner as a 1,000-yard rusher in 1985.

Byner excelled in the biggest games. He earned the tag as "heart and soul" of Browns playoff teams from 1985 through '88. But his fumble in the 1987 AFC championship game in Denver is among the most heartbreaking moments in Browns lore.

Byner had 120 yards receiving and 67 rushing in a rollicking slugfest with John Elway's Broncos. He was heading into the end zone for what would have been the tying touchdown with 65 seconds remaining when cornerback Jeremiah Castille stripped him of the ball at the Denver three.

The Broncos prevailed, 38-33, to turn back the Browns' Super Bowl bid a second year in a row.

The silhouette of Byner kneeling in the end zone without the ball as fans in Mile High Stadium celebrated is an image still etched in the minds of teammates.

Byner earned praise for standing up to the mistake in front of the media immediately after the game. In truth, he hid his personal anguish for years.

"It changed the way I played the game some," Byner said almost 16 years later. "Nobody knew. It was pulling on me. It was kicking my tail, to tell you the truth. I was basically slowly rotting inside. It was killing me.

"A lot of fans in Cleveland were devastated by that, which I know and I understand. But nobody was hurt more than me."

The following year, Byner committed back-to-back personal fouls in a wild-card playoff game the Browns lost by one point. Three months later, he was traded to Washington for a nondescript back named Mike Oliphant.

"At that point, it was almost like Ralph Branca or Bill Buckner," said Ernie Accorsi, director of football operations, referring to other athletes who made infamous errors. "There had just been too much, and it was time. In retrospect, it was a

Earnest Byner (© Brockway Sports Photos)

mistake. It's hard to have the objectivity when you're in the emotions of the moment."

Byner went on to lead the Redskins in rushing for three seasons and gained over 1,000 yards in two of them. He earned a Super Bowl ring with them in 1991.

The pain of "the fumble" followed Byner to Washington. He said he finally exorcised it by forgiving himself in writing.

"I wrote a journal, wrote about the play and the game, wrote about forgiving myself for making a mistake," he said. "I was hard on myself, always was. I guess that's one reason I was able to continue to play as long as I did. I took my game personally and seriously."

After Accorsi left the Browns, Byner returned to Cleveland as a free agent in 1994 because coach Bill Belichick needed his leadership in the locker room.

"Some of the fans probably wanted me to get the hell out of town for a while," Byner said. "But when I came back, I was welcomed with open arms."

The 1995 season was the darkest year in Browns history, as the team played out the string as a lame-duck franchise waiting to be moved to Baltimore. Byner provided the lone highlight after the announcement. Amid a funereal atmosphere in the final game in old Cleveland Municipal Stadium, Byner rushed for 121 yards in a victory over Cincinnati.

"It was poetic justice," he said.

He concluded the eerie day by circling the perimeter of the grandstands and touching the hands of fans in a farewell gesture.

Byner joined Art Modell's Ravens in Baltimore for two more seasons. He became the first player honored in the Ravens' "Ring of Honor." He also was selected for the Washington Redskins all-time team.

After retirement, Byner took the position of Ravens director of player development, a role that required him to counsel and console players. By then, he considered himself an expert on dealing with pain.

"Pain gives you a lot of wisdom," he said.

KEVIN MACK

Every great Browns era was powered by a great running back. Kevin Mack fueled the Browns' playoff teams from 1985 to '89.

"When he first got there and got down to run—he was such a big guy that you figured he was just a power back, and he ran a 4.38 in the 40," recalled teammate Dave Puzzuoli. "A lot of us just never saw a big dude run that fast before."

Quiet and shy, Mack was the last person convinced he was worthy of joining the tradition of great Browns backs started by Marion Motley.

He played one year in the United States Football League because he didn't think he was good enough for the NFL. Upon joining the Browns, Mack needed constant encouragement that he belonged. He got it from running back Earnest Byner and coach Marty Schottenheimer.

"We had a preseason game in Buffalo and I can remember Marty telling me, 'You're better than 90 percent of the guys out here. You shouldn't feel intimidated,'" Mack said.

Mack responded by shattering Jim Brown's rookie rushing record with 1,104 yards in 1985. He joined Byner [1,002 yards] as only the third pair of NFL teammates to rush for 1,000 yards the same year.

"It came a little too easy. I was surprised," Mack said.

Mack never reached 1,000 yards again. Injuries, sometimes inflicted by his bruising running style, caused him to miss playing time in two of the next three years. After the 1988 season, Mack lost Byner, his best friend and personal mentor, who was traded to Washington.

A few months later in June of 1989, the team was blindsided when Mack was arrested in his car in a drug-infested neighborhood on Cleveland's east side. The following six months would be a living hell for him.

Mack had a rehabilitation stay at the Cleveland Clinic and then was suspended four games by the NFL. During the suspension, he had surgery on an injured knee. Finally, he was sentenced to six months in prison after pleading guilty to one count of cocaine abuse. He was released on shock probation in November after serving 30 days in two different institutions.

"It was a serious wake-up call," Mack said. "Being a young kid, you feel you can get away with anything, that you're bulletproof. I had a lot of tough things to get through, but it was a very helpful learning experience. With Earnest traded, I pretty much felt on my own. I had to dig deep and get with the program, pretty much grow up and be a man."

When Mack rejoined his teammates in the middle of a playoff push, he was riddled with guilt.

"I felt like I let a lot of people down," he said. "I didn't think there was anything I could do to make up for what I did and the position I put my team in. There was a lot of doubt and guilt."

Mack slowly rounded into playing shape, setting up a dramatic night in Houston's Astrodome in the season's 16th game. With the playoffs riding on the outcome, Mack climaxed a winning drive when he literally carried three Houston defenders on his back on a four-yard touchdown run with 39 seconds left.

Kevin Mack (© Brockway Sports Photos)

"That's the greatest run of that distance I've ever seen in my life," team executive Ernie Accorsi said 14 years later.

After the game, Mack sat on a padded table in a trainer's room away from his teammates. He cried uncontrollably as owner Art Modell clenched his arms around him.

"It felt like a weight had been lifted off me and that I had finally given something back," Mack said.

His career with the Browns would end as quietly as it began.

New coach Bill Belichick took over in 1991 and dismantled the team Mack had known and loved. Mack announced his retirement in the 1993 training camp, then changed his mind. Belichick reluctantly agreed to bring him back. He relegated Mack to the "scout team" in practice for weeks.

"I can vividly recall practicing against the defense and just creaming guys—defensive lineme—and he got pissed one day and yelled out, 'Get him out of there before he hurts somebody,'" Mack said. "At that point, I realized he wasn't going to put me back on the field."

In his last game in Cleveland Stadium, Mack did not play a down on offense. Belichick defied the home crowd that chanted "We want Mack" and would not let him carry the ball one last time.

ERNIE ACCORSI

Ernie Accorsi was smitten with the quarterback position as a teenager when he saw the first appearance of Johnny Unitas in an exhibition game in 1953. "He just gave off an aura," Accorsi said of the Hall of Fame legend. They would become close friends.

Accorsi's infatuation with the quarterback position served him well when his career shifted from sportswriting to public relations and finally to NFL executive. One of his last acts as Baltimore Colts general manager was to select John Elway with the first pick of the 1983 draft even though Elway insisted he didn't want to play for bumbling Colts owner Bob Irsay.

A few days later, Irsay traded Elway's rights to Denver without Accorsi's knowledge. The transaction reverberated for decades, changing the course of NFL history in several cities.

Irsay abandoned Baltimore and moved the Colts to Indianapolis prior to the following season. Accorsi resigned from the Colts and joined the Browns. Ultimately, the Browns lost three times to Elway's Denver Broncos in the AFC championship game in the late 1980s.

But those were fun times for the Browns, and they were jump-started by Accorsi's master stroke of obtaining his Unitas-Boardman, Ohio-bred quarterback Bernie Kosar. It was an innovative plan that stamped the Browns as a franchise to be reckoned with in the 1980s.

Kosar was contemplating leaving the University of Miami with two years' eligibility left because he was in the unique position of graduating in three academic years, rather than four.

"I read a line in a paper somewhere that he was thinking of coming out, which was unheard of," Accorsi recalled. "Jim Houston [former Browns linebacker] was a friend of the Kosar family, and he called Art Modell and told him Bernie wanted to play for the Browns."

Accorsi immediately phoned Joel Bussert, a friend in the NFL office, and asked him to clarify the NFL draft rule for him.

"You're going down a road that's going to cause a lot of trouble," Bussert told him.

"It was uncharted waters," Accorsi recalled. "The more I investigated it, the more I realized he could do this."

The problem was the Browns held the No. 7 position in the draft and Minnesota, sitting No. 3, wanted Kosar, too. Accorsi tried to leapfrog Minnesota with a trade with Houston, at No. 2, but Oilers general manager Ladd Herzeg asked for the moon.

"It was then that it dawned upon me there was another way to get this done," Accorsi said.

Accorsi and the Kosar family understood that Kosar was in a unique position to manipulate the NFL draft process. He could wait till he graduated in June before declaring his intention to enter the NFL. The league would have to hold a special supplemental draft in that case, repeating the order of the regular draft.

With this in mind, Accorsi swung a deal with Buffalo, which held the first position if a supplemental draft were held.

"I'll never forget," Accorsi said. "Ladd called me that day and said, 'I just want to inform you we've traded Kosar's rights to the Vikings.' I said, 'No, you didn't. You may have traded your choice, but I just want to tell you we've traded for Buffalo's first pick in the supplemental draft.'"

Houston and Minnesota protested to NFL commissioner Pete Rozelle. Rozelle froze both trades pending a hearing in his office. By the day of Rozelle's ruling, thousands of fans bombarded *The Plain Dealer* telephones to learn of the verdict. The onslaught of calls blew out the newspaper's telephone system.

Rozelle ruled that Kosar could, in fact, choose his team by choosing which draft he would enter. The whole episode caused a stir in the NFL and resulted in the loophole eventually being closed. Now, the supplemental draft is held as a weighted lottery in which each team has a mathematical chance to claim the first pick.

Accorsi assigned Kosar jersey No. 19 to honor Unitas. With Kosar as quarterback, the Browns reached the playoffs five consecutive years—only to be denied the Super Bowl three times by Elway's team.

"When you're involved in it, the intensity of it year to year, sometimes you lose sight of what a great time it was," Accorsi said. "When you realize it 10 or 15 years later, five years in a row in the playoffs was a great accomplishment. They were great years in a great football town in a great old stadium. I cherish those memories."

Matt Bahr

Matt Bahr won one Super Bowl ring kicking for the Pittsburgh Steelers in 1979 and another with the New York Giants in 1990. But it was the nine years in between with the Browns that he remembers most fondly.

"They really were a family," he said. "The guys genuinely enjoyed one another's company and went out together. I don't recall any other team being that way, with the constant camaraderie that went on with the entire team. My time with the Browns was really old-school, classic football."

Nobody knew Cleveland Municipal Stadium's capricious winds and uneven field better than Bahr. Despite consistently horrendous kicking conditions, Bahr actually had a higher field goal percentage in games in Cleveland than every place else.

"Maybe because the weather was so rotten a lot of the time, I ended up concentrating better," he said. "I actually found myself struggling on artificial turf because the conditions were too perfect.

"The pride I took in Cleveland was in just kicking on that muddy field. That open end of the stadium was the demise of so many kickers, because unless you stood in the end zone, you couldn't feel the wind that was blowing like a hurricane straight across the field."

Bahr could be quirky, playfully posing questions to teammates such as "Why do we drive on a parkway and park on a driveway?" But he was respected as a kicker who made clutch kicks and was willing to throw his body at a returner to make a tackle.

One such tackle saved a touchdown in an important win against his former Pittsburgh Steelers in 1986. Bahr was having a career season at the time. He tore knee ligaments and had to sit out for over a year.

That the injury occurred against the Steelers was an added insult. Bahr never forgave Pittsburgh coach Chuck Noll for cutting him from his hometown team in his second season.

"I don't know if anybody ever understood Chuck," Bahr said. "He was an enigma. When he was done with you, that was it."

Bahr never employed an agent. Former Browns executive Ernie Accorsi recalled Bahr "negotiating" a new contract in his office.

"He has this little piece of paper with the figures $140,000 and $150,000 written on it and he slips it across the desk to me, real sheepishly," Accorsi said. "He says, 'This is what I'd like to have.'

"I look at it and say, 'I'm not giving you this.' He says, 'I know, I'm just asking.'

"I had written down $160,000 and $170,000 and I said, 'That's what you're getting.'

"When I made my list of top 10 favorite players, he's on it," Accorsi said.

Bahr wound up fourth on the Browns' all-time scoring list and third in field goals. Never once did he so much as raise a fist after a successful kick.

"I always jogged off the field the same way whether I made it or missed it," he said. "That comes from hearing my dad say, 'Act like you've done it before. And always remember, you're not out there alone.'"

BERNIE KOSAR

Situated between Cleveland and Pittsburgh, Boardman, Ohio, was a bipolar football town in the early 1980s. Half the residents rooted for the Browns, and the other half rooted for the archrival Steelers.

It was a good thing for the Browns that Bernie Kosar grew up a fan of Brian Sipe and not Terry Bradshaw. For when it came time for the precocious quarterback to choose his NFL team—a unique circumstance that stirred great controversy—he stood up and announced to a disbelieving sports world that he wanted to play in Cleveland.

"Kosar just injected the whole region with pride," recalled Ernie Accorsi, who was the point man in the Browns' secret plan to acquire Kosar in 1985. "He was one of their own. I remember the exhilaration of getting him."

As a true freshman at the University of Miami, Kosar engineered a shocking upset of Nebraska to claim the mythical national championship. Returning to his hometown team at a time when it wasn't popular made Kosar an instant regional sports icon.

It was a responsibility that he treasured and held tightly.

"When he first came in, I thought, 'Who is this kid who everybody thinks is a savior?'" recalled cornerback Hanford Dixon. "He proved himself to be a gutsy gunslinger."

Bernie Kosar (© Brockway Sports Photos)

A gangly 6'5" and 210 pounds, Kosar threw with an unorthodox, sidearm motion and moved with an awkward gait. His throws often looked bad. But Kosar's uncanny football mind and riveting vision of the field created passing lanes that others couldn't see.

"I always felt he had a unique style that he made work," said Gary Danielson, Kosar's mentor his first four years in the NFL. "And I think [coaches and teammates] gained confidence in his toughness and his ability to think his way through things.

"The secret to Bernie was his broad vision. He was very disciplined in his thinking, he was very committed to what he thought was right, he was as tough physically as you had to be, and he was a workaholic."

One sign of Kosar's maturity came to light in his first season when he stated after his first playoff loss: "Age is no excuse for failure."

Coaches usually met resistance when they held him back.

"He played sandlot ball," Dixon said. "A lot of coaches didn't like that, which was crazy, because all Bernie Kosar did was win ballgames."

Kosar started in his first playoff game as a rookie at age 22. He led the Browns to five consecutive playoff appearances, beginning in 1985. The run included four division titles and three appearances in the AFC championship game.

Typically in his career, Kosar would stumble before succeeding. He fumbled the first snap in his first NFL game, and then completed seven passes in a row. His two interceptions dug a 10-point deficit against the Jets in a playoff game in the 1986 season. He made it up in the final four minutes and won the game in two overtimes, the Browns' first postseason victory in 17 years.

Alas, Kosar could not get the Browns past Denver in three AFC title game duels with John Elway.

By the time Bill Belichick took over as coach in 1991, Kosar's physical limitations were becoming evident. An elbow injury suffered in the 1988 season opener in Kansas City took a toll on his arm strength, and poor offensive lines accentuated his immobility.

"I think what changed him the most was the hit in Kansas City," Danielson said. "I don't think he was ever the same."

Kosar and Belichick had a mutual respect early on, but friction developed as they disagreed about offensive style and play calling. After two seasons, Belichick acquired strong-armed Vinny Testaverde, Kosar's friend and former rival at Miami.

In 1993, differences between Kosar and Belichick escalated to the point of no return. They squabbled on the sidelines and in meetings. There was no physical confrontation, but Belichick believed his authority was threatened.

The coach convinced owner Art Modell it was in the team's best interest to release Kosar in the middle of the season with the Browns tied for first place with a 5-3 record. Testaverde was recovering from a shoulder separation at the time.

"I think both people were at fault in their own ways," said a member of the Browns front office a decade later. "I don't know what could have been done to avoid it."

Kosar was immediately signed by the Dallas Cowboys for a guaranteed $1 million. He filled in for Troy Aikman in the NFC championship game and contributed to a win over San Francisco, sending the Cowboys into the Super Bowl.

The release from the Browns was traumatic to their fans and to Kosar, but it did enable him to earn a Super Bowl ring in Dallas.

GARY DANIELSON

All of Cleveland was abuzz in 1985 about Bernie Kosar, the kid quarterback who manipulated the NFL rules to play for his hometown team. Gary Danielson kind of sneaked into town under Kosar's shadow.

Danielson joined the Browns in a trade with the Detroit Lions the day after the draft. He was 33, fiercely proud and competitive, and full of wit and wisdom.

"We all agreed we needed a veteran to play and groom Kosar," recalled Ernie Accorsi, the director of football operations. "Our first choice was Steve Grogan of New England, but we couldn't get him.

"The guy who talked me into Gary Danielson was Ted Marchibroda. He described Gary Danielson to a tee. Gary became the perfect guy."

Danielson could have been traded to Seattle, but the Lions accommodated his wish to go to Cleveland.

"When I first got there, they told me what they expected," Danielson said. "What they wanted was someone to play that first half of the year. They felt the team was ready to win. And if I went in there and did well, I would play.

"We talked about the fact that Bernie needed to practice, too. I was comfortable with that. Even if I was the starter, Bernie could still practice half the time.

"And they wanted someone who understood football and communicated well with him. Bernie was much brighter and more football savvy than I realized."

The two hit it off as mentor and student and football buddies.

Danielson got the Browns off to a 2-2 start, then suffered a torn rotator cuff in his right throwing shoulder in the fifth game. He postponed surgery to be able to play if the team stayed in the playoff hunt. It did.

With the Browns at 5-6 and Kosar sputtering, coach Marty Schottenheimer called on Danielson to start a crucial game against division rival Cincinnati.

"I threw my shoulder out in the first half and Marty said, 'I think we can win this game if we just keep running,'" Danielson said. "I didn't throw one pass the whole second half until I audibled and hit a long pass to Clarence Weathers [for a 72-yard touchdown]. I got hit and my shoulder popped out again."

Danielson threw seven passes total, completing four, and the Browns won, 24-6, to even their record at 6-6. Danielson prepared to start the next game against the New York Giants, but he couldn't throw in pregame warmups.

Ahead at halftime, 21-20, Schottenheimer said to Danielson, "I've got to put you in. Our team needs a lift."

The Giants pulled ahead, 33-21, before Danielson brought the Browns back. Getting smashed by linebacker and cornerback blitzes after nearly every throw, he led two touchdown drives in the final quarter.

"Every time I threw, the rotator cuff popped out. I had to keep slipping it back in," he remembered.

Danielson was in so much pain he had to leave the field before the Browns scored their winning touchdown. Kosar reentered the game and handed off to Earnest Byner for the winning score and a dramatic 35-33 victory.

In the locker room, Danielson accepted congratulations with his left hand. He could not raise his right arm above his hip. He didn't play again that year and had shoulder surgery. The Browns won their division with an 8-8 record and lost to Miami in the playoffs.

The following summer, he was beating out Kosar for the starting job in preseason and suffered a broken ankle in the last exhibition game.

By the 1987 season, Kosar was firmly in charge as the starter. But an NFL players' strike threatened team chemistry. In the third week of the strike, Browns management asked Danielson to cross the picket line for a key division game in Cincinnati.

"They felt it was better for the radical players to be upset with me rather than Bernie," he said.

With Danielson and seven other veteran players back in uniform, the Browns crushed the Bengals, 34-0, and won their third straight division title.

"I think my most important role with the Browns was I was somebody for Bernie to bounce off his ideas," Danielson said. "He was a genius-level quarterback in his mind. He needed somebody to talk to that he respected. He needed a friend and a confidante.

"I know a lot of people felt I helped create a more radical Bernie. That was not the case. I was just somebody for him to talk to."

HANFORD DIXON
AND FRANK MINNIFIELD

Cornerbacks Hanford Dixon and Frank Minnifield joined the Browns via different avenues in the 1980s. Dixon was a first-round draft choice in 1981. Minnifield was signed as a free agent from the United States Football League in 1984.

Together for six seasons, they formed the best pair of bump-and-run cornerbacks in the NFL.

Coach Sam Rutigliano had both players only for eight games. Defensive coordinator Marty Schottenheimer succeeded as coach and built his defense around them.

"For maybe a seven- to eight-year run, no one had a better perimeter defense," Rutigliano said. "Minnifield was a great little competitor, a smart guy. Dixon was a pain in the ass. The only way you could coach Dixon was to say, 'I don't think you're a very good player. You can do a lot better.' You'd always have to insult him."

Dixon and Minnifield grew inseparable off the field, often brainstorming projects on their own. One involved Minnifield's knowledge of computers. He and Dixon were the first players

Hanford Dixon (© Brockway Sports Photos)

on the Browns, if not the entire NFL, to download game film onto computers and use laptops to study opponents.

But their greatest legacy was in creating the "dawg" identity for the Browns and renaming the open-end bleacher grandstands in old Cleveland Stadium "the Dawg Pound."

Both players dispute assertions by nose tackle Dave Puzzuoli that the late Eddie Johnson was the first to call their teammates "dawgs."

"That was the most ridiculous thing I heard," Dixon said. "The Dawgs came from me."

The Dawgs were born in the 1985 Browns training camp at Lakeland Community College.

"We didn't have a great defensive line, and I was just thinking of a way to get those guys going," Dixon said. "I started barking at them. The fans at Lakeland were so close to the fields, they'd hear me and Minnie barking, and they'd bark back."

Minnifield said he and Dixon christened the Dawg Pound when they personally hung a banner in the bleachers prior to the team's first home exhibition game in August of 1985.

"Me and Hanford made it up and we put it in the stands ourselves," Minnifield said.

Dixon and Minnifield popularized the identity by barking during practices and games. They even barked during interviews on radio and television.

By the dawn of the 1986 season, everyone was referring to the Browns' defense as the Dawgs. Fans got into the act by dressing in dog masks and carrying dog attire, such as giant bones and boxes of biscuits.

The following year, Minnifield hatched a marketing idea. He had the four members of the starting defensive secondary pose in black tuxedos on the steps of the federal courthouse

Frank Minnifield (© Brockway Sports Photos)

downtown. Each held a different menacing breed of dog on a leash. The poster was titled, "The Last Dawgs of Defense."

"I'd been calling Hanford for weeks to tell him what day we would shoot the photograph for it, and the day before we shoot, he's in Mississippi," Minnifield said. "I told him we were going to shoot it without him if he wasn't there at two o'clock. Hanford drove all night long from Mississippi to be there. And he made it on time."

The Dawgs became the identity of the entire team. In a game in 1989—John Elway's first appearance in Cleveland since his famous 98-yard drive in the 1986 AFC championship—fans in the Dawg Pound pelted Elway and his Bronco teammates with a barrage of dog biscuits and other weightier projectiles. The game referee ultimately moved the Broncos to the other end of the field and threatened to forfeit the game if it didn't stop.

The barking and costuming connected the team to its fans.

"It was real simple," Minnifield said. "Me and Hanford realized real soon after it took off that it gave us an advantage. It became a distraction for the other team. It interrupted their preparation for the game.

"The Dawg Pound proved to be an unbelievable experience for me and an unbelievable advantage for our defensive team. The energy that the city of Cleveland can create and did create, it was … I don't know … like standing on top of a pile of precious material."

Sometime in the three years of the Browns' hiatus from the NFL from 1996 through '98, the NFL copyrighted the Dawg Pound, blocking Dixon's hope of cashing in. And when the team was reborn in 1999 in a new stadium, "Dawg Pound" appeared on the railing in front of the grandstand.

"Let's face it, the league was just sharper than we were," Dixon said.

CARL (BIG DADDY) HAIRSTON

More than a dozen years after his playing career ended, Carl Hairston answers the phone in his office: "Big Daddy here."

He was given the nickname by strength coach Dave (Red Man) Redding shortly after joining the Browns in 1984 in a trade with the Philadelphia Eagles.

"I hated it," Hairston said. "I remember chasing Red Man in the weight room with a five-pound weight to throw at him. I took it the wrong way. I thought people looked at 'Big Daddy' as a bad guy, a drug dealer, something like that."

In truth, Hairston was one of the Browns' all-time good guys.

He joined the Browns at age 32 with his knee in a cast recovering from surgery. The trade invigorated him. Hairston became a driving force—and a mentor to young defensive linemen—on five consecutive Browns playoff teams beginning in 1985.

"He was in his early 30s and he looked like my uncle, like he was 48 at the time," said teammate Dave Puzzuoli. "He was a classic, old-school pro. He was all about football and team camaraderie. The cat was doing things on the field that you wouldn't think he should be able to do.

"Sometimes there are guys who just have a good time and don't lift weights really hard and still kick the tar out of people. That was Big Daddy. He was something out of a *Saturday Night*

Live skit. The more scotch and waters he drank, the stronger he was. He would go against these steroid guys benching 500 pounds and he'd be out partying the night before, and he'd destroy them. He was a genius on the field."

In 1979, Hairston led the NFC with 15 sacks with the Eagles. He led the Browns in '86 and '87 with eight each season.

Befitting his happy-go-lucky personality, Hairston gained his most notoriety for accepting a lateral from linebacker Clay Matthews after an interception and trundling 40 yards to set up a touchdown in a key division victory against Cincinnati in 1987.

"That play still pops into my mind now and then," Hairston said. "I still remember looking at the sideline and seeing the guys laughing. You never knew what Clay was going to do. When I saw him turn his head, I thought, 'Please don't throw this ball to me.'"

A less funny moment in his career happened a year earlier, when John Elway drove 98 yards in the AFC championship game to deny the Browns a trip to the Super Bowl. Recurring highlights of the game-tying touchdown pass show Hairston's right hand barely missing the ball as it left Elway's hand.

"I could feel the wind of the ball go by the tip of my fingers," Hairston said. "I might have tipped it just a smidgeon."

Hairston left the Browns for Arizona in 1990. Upon retirement, he joined the Cardinals' scouting staff. He moved into coaching in 1995 under Marty Schottenheimer with the Kansas City Chiefs. He joined Dick Vermeil, who coached him Philadelphia, in St. Louis, and then rejoined him with the Chiefs.

Hairston played in one Super Bowl and coached in one— both times under Vermeil.

"I just wish we could have won one of those championships with the Browns and gone to the Super Bowl," he said.

SAM CLANCY

He had the long arms of an NBA rebounder, and that's exactly what Sam Clancy intended to be. He turned out to be a serviceable pass rusher for the Browns on four consecutive playoff seasons in the 1980s. And he never played a down of college football.

Clancy is the only Browns player to have played for basketball coach Bobby Knight.

"I've never been around a kid better than he was," Knight once said. "You could beat a hell of a lot of people with Sam Clancy playing for you."

A four-year letter winner in basketball at the University of Pittsburgh, Clancy made the United States team coached by Knight that won the gold medal in the 1979 Pan American Games. Included on that team were future NBA stars Kevin McHale, Isiah Thomas, Mike Woodson and Ralph Sampson.

During the tournament, Knight created an international incident by allegedly punching a police officer in San Juan, Puerto Rico.

"Bobby Knight didn't slap the guy," said Clancy, an eyewitness to the incident. "He pushed the guy on the side of his face.

"Here's what led up to that:

"We came about a half-hour early to practice and another team was on the court. A policeman said they didn't want us in there watching their practice. It was pouring rain and our bus left. Bobby Knight said, 'Fine,' so we stood out in the pouring rain hugging the walls after the bus left.

"Bobby Knight told the policeman, 'We don't want anyone walking in on our practice, either.' About 20 minutes into our practice, here comes the Brazilian team walking through. Well, Bobby Knight wasn't going to take that shit."

At Pitt, Clancy was swayed to the football team by coach Jackie Sherrill his senior season, but a sprained ankle two weeks into practice ended his football career. A new basketball coach told him to choose between the sports, and Clancy stayed with his first love.

Clancy was drafted in the third round by the NBA Phoenix Suns and later played in the Continental Basketball Association. A friend of Sherrill's with the NFL Seattle Seahawks persuaded the team to draft Clancy in the seventh round of the 1982 NFL draft.

"I wanted to be a tight end, but what you hear about rookie woes in training camp, I was a prime example," he said. "I was blown away by the offensive terminology."

Clancy was switched to defensive end. He came to the Browns after two years in the United States Football League, where he turned in 16 sacks in one season with the Pittsburgh Maulers and four playing with Reggie White with the Memphis Showboats.

Clancy had 14 sacks in four seasons with the Browns. They made the playoffs each year, but lost to Denver's John Elway twice in the AFC championship game.

"I know people in Cleveland hate Elway as a player, and I did, too," Clancy said. "But, man, I probably respect him more than any quarterback I ever had to face."

Clancy played five more seasons with the Indianapolis Colts before moving into the coaching ranks as a defensive line specialist with several teams.

Clancy named each of his children a derivative of Sam— Sam Jr., Samantha, Samario and Samarcus. Sam Jr. grew to 6'7" and was a draft choice of the Philadelphia 76ers after playing at Southern Cal.

"I tried to get Sam to play for Bobby Knight at Indiana, but he was scared," Clancy said, laughing. "If he had my heart, with his skills, he'd be unstoppable."

DAVE PUZZUOLI

Dave Puzzuoli had 16 sacks in five seasons as a backup nose tackle for the Browns in the late 1980s. One of them should have been bronzed in history as the play that vaulted the Browns into their first Super Bowl.

The Browns were trying to defend a 20-13 lead on their home field in the AFC championship game following the 1986 season. John Elway had taken his Denver Broncos from the two-yard line to the Browns' 40.

On the ninth play of the drive, Puzzuoli was inserted for starter Bob Golic to give the Browns a better pass rush.

"That was one of the few plays where we were in a pass-rush mindset," Puzzuoli recalled. "We brought four people. Clay Matthews came from the right side. Clay forced the sack. It was one of the rare times it worked the way it's drawn up. Elway had to step up, and that's where I had him."

Puzzuoli buried Elway for an eight-yard loss, setting up third and 18 at the Broncos' 48-yard line.

"I just jumped right up and celebrated," Puzzuoli said. "The crowd was so loud, you couldn't hear yourself think, so there was no sense saying anything to Elway because he couldn't hear a word I said."

Puzzuoli was immediately removed from the field by coach Marty Schottenheimer. The conservative coach chose to flood the secondary with eight defensive backs and rush only three linemen on the next play.

"When I came back to the sideline, we thought we were going to the Bowl," Puzzuoli said. "We looked at each other like, 'We actually did it.' That was the look in our eyes. Obviously, it was a little premature."

Elway then pulled off the play of his career. As he surveyed the Browns' defense from the shotgun formation, the center snap caromed off the hip of receiver Steve Watson, who was in motion. Elway picked the ball off the ground and completed a 20-yard pass to Mark Jackson for a first down.

"When that ball bounced off Watson, if it falls on the ground and we recover it, the game's over," Puzzuoli said. "And the greatest thing would have been the fact that the fans—the crowd noise—would have caused that. Essentially, the crowd would have gotten us to the Super Bowl."

It was not to be. Elway completed the 98-yard drive in five more plays. The Broncos won it in overtime on a field goal. It is one of the Browns' all-time painful losses.

Puzzouli's sack was the only play he was on the field in what instantly became known as "The Drive."

Earlier that season, Puzzuoli earned some good-natured ribbing from teammates while subbing occasionally as a blocking back on offense. When fullback Earnest Byner went down with an ankle injury, the 260-pound Puzzuoli was chosen by coaches to fill the role made famous by William (the Refrigerator) Perry of the Chicago Bears.

"The first time they used me was in a game in the Metrodome in Minnesota," Puzzuoli recalled. "I was so jazzed, so totally overextended, I went into the hole and was willing to take on everyone and anyone who showed up. And no one showed up and I just dove to the ground. I was just like a javelin going into the ground."

In the 16th game, the Browns were pummeling the San Diego Chargers by the score of 47-17. Teammates goaded Puzzuoli into asking Schottenheimer to give him the ball on a handoff.

"I figured he'd be laughing a little bit and I said, 'Hey Coach, how about giving me the ball?' He just looked at me and said, 'Hey, Puz, how about if you don't play at all?'"

DON ROGERS

Sam Rutigliano and Art Modell talked of "saving lives" through the organization's Inner Circle drug program in the early 1980s. But not even the most progressive self-help program in the NFL at the time could save the life of Don Rogers.

In 1985, Rogers was the Browns' No. 1 draft choice. Affable, dedicated and talented, the free safety from UCLA was seen as the missing element in a defense maturing into one of the AFC's elite.

In June of 1986, Rogers was dead of a cocaine overdose at the age of 23. He died after his own bachelor party the night before he was to be married in his hometown of Sacramento, California.

Teammate Hanford Dixon made the trip from Cleveland to Sacramento the day of the party and attended it at a local nightclub.

"I can still see him the last night before he died," Dixon said more than 15 years later. "I saw Donnie leave, and then I left because I was tired after a long flight. Next thing I knew, I was woken up by somebody telling me we had to go to the hospital because Donnie had ODed and he was not going to make it. I thought somebody was playing a prank on me."

A Sacramento County coroner's investigator told a reporter that Rogers had enough drugs in him "to kill an elephant."

When news of the tragedy spread to club officials and players scattered at their off-season homes, feelings of shock and emptiness devastated the organization.

"I was knocked off my feet," recalled cornerback Frank Minnifield. "He was a real progressive person, a person that was looking down the road talking about owning companies, trying to help mom and dad. That was his whole life—just to get back home and help everybody."

Rogers's memory stayed with the team, even though Modell elected not to memorialize him because of the circumstances of his death.

When the Browns' defense permitted the 98-yard drive by Denver quarterback John Elway in the AFC championship game later that year, the "what-ifs" were unavoidable.

"I always felt that if Donnie Rogers hadn't died, he would have made a play on that drive," said Ernie Accorsi, the director of football operations.

"I remember Donnie told me after his rookie season, 'I'm taking the secondary over next year.' And he had the personality to do it. He was so happy-go-lucky, such an upbeat guy. I just always felt that somewhere in that drive he would've made a play."

The Browns fell one victory short of making the Super Bowl following the 1986, '87 and '89 seasons—years in which Rogers would be in his athletic prime.

"If we go into those three games against Denver with Don Rogers, we're so much better," Minnifield said.

MARK MOSELEY

The Browns couldn't celebrate their biggest victory of the 1986 season, an overtime thriller against the rival Pittsburgh Steelers. They needed a kicker after Matt Bahr tore knee ligaments on a leg-whip tackle of Pittsburgh return specialist Lupe Sanchez in overtime.

After the game, Art Modell paced in his owner's box in Municipal Stadium and fretted about Bahr's replacement.

"Who in the world are we gonna find now?" Modell demanded of Ernie Accorsi, his top aide.

Accorsi looked at the television playing in Modell's suite and saw retired Washington Redskins kicker Mark Moseley doing postgame commentary for *The NFL Today* on CBS.

"That guy right there," Accorsi said, pointing to the TV screen.

Modell made an immediate call to the CBS studio in New York. During a commercial break, Moseley was handed a note that Art Modell was on the phone and wanted to talk to him.

On the set, Jimmy (the Greek) Snyder laughed and said, "Aw, we get those cranks all the time." He grabbed the note, wadded it up and threw it in the trash.

When Moseley got home, a message was left for him to call Modell. After they finally hooked up, Moseley was on a plane to Cleveland the next afternoon. The next day, he beat out three kickers in a tryout and was thrown into the fire of the Browns' first real chase for the Super Bowl.

Moseley, 38, was the Redskins' all-time scoring leader and held every career kicking record for the franchise when the team cut him a month earlier. He was the last of the NFL's straight-on kickers and had been for five years running.

"I came in during Thanksgiving week and I was staying in a motel," Moseley recalled. "Don Cockroft called and invited me to his house for Thanksgiving Day dinner. That was really a great thing. I'd always looked up to Don during my career."

In his first game, Moseley strapped on his usual five layers of socks on his right foot and kicked a field goal in overtime to defeat the Houston Oilers.

The Browns rolled into the playoffs on the strength of five straight victories. In their first playoff game, the Browns had to stage a frantic, fourth-quarter comeback against the New York Jets in Municipal Stadium.

Moseley sent the game into overtime with a 22-yard field goal. But he stunningly missed the winning kick from a few yards longer in the first overtime.

"We were right in the middle of the biggest mudhole you've ever seen in your life," Moseley said. "You couldn't even stand up in it.

"We got the ball back in the second overtime and were driving down and [coach] Marty Schottenheimer called me over and asked what we should do about the field. I said we've got to stop short of getting real close so that we're not in that mess out there. It was impossible to get any footing."

Moseley kicked the game winner from 27 yards to send the Browns into the AFC championship game against the Denver Broncos.

"The Redskins were playing the New York Giants for the NFC championship the same day," Moseley remembered. "There were as many Washington reporters at the Cleveland game because everybody thought I'd be playing my old team in the Super Bowl and it was a huge story in Washington."

It didn't happen. The Browns and Redskins both lost. Moseley retired after the Browns drafted a kicker the following spring.

"I'm proud of being a part of Browns history," Moseley said. "That was a fun time in my life and a real good way to finish out."

DON STROCK

There's never been another Browns season like the one in 1988.

At the start, they considered quarterback their deepest position. But injuries wiped out their top three passers, and the

Browns were forced to call on Don Strock, the NFL's preeminent relief specialist, to save their season.

The injuries started in Game 1 as Bernie Kosar went down with a sprained right elbow. Backup Gary Danielson broke his left ankle in Game 2. The Browns still had Mike Pagel to take over as starter, but their playoff hopes hinged on signing another veteran quarterback—just in case something happened to Pagel.

Strock, 38, had served 15 years with the Miami Dolphins as backup to Bob Griese, Earl Morrall, David Woodley and Dan Marino. His relationship with the Dolphins was severed by a contract dispute.

The Browns tracked down Strock at Doral Country Club in south Florida, where he essentially was enjoying retirement as a celebrity greeter. Getting him to agree to a contract was "unbearable," according to Ernie Accorsi, Browns director of football operations at the time.

"Jerry Kapstein, his agent, had us by the throat," Accorsi recalled. "It was the toughest negotiation I can remember in Cleveland. Here's a guy who was playing golf at Doral and we couldn't get him signed."

Nobody thought Strock would see much time, anyway.

Pagel said: "You've got to say the odds are in my favor of staying healthy. I've seen the No. 1 quarterback get hurt. I've seen the No. 2 quarterback get hurt. Three in a row? C'mon."

Four games later, Pagel suffered a separated shoulder making a touchdown-saving tackle against Seattle after a blocked field goal. Enter Strock.

"I've never seen anything like this before," wailed owner Art Modell. "I get worried when I see someone lift a wine glass."

At 3-3, the Browns' playoff hopes were in the hands of Strock, who hadn't started a game in five years.

"He's got to play against that great Philadelphia defense," Accorsi recalled, "and he's at practice, with that pot belly, tanned all over. And [coach] Marty [Schottenheimer] says to me, 'I don't know if this is good or bad, but Strock doesn't give a damn.'"

Wearing a cheat sheet of 55 plays strapped to his left wrist, Strock stepped in and defeated Philadelphia, 19-3, on two touchdown passes in the second half.

Kosar returned the next week. But in the 15th game in Miami, Kosar was knocked out again with a bruised knee. In his first appearance in Miami in a visitor's uniform, Strock threw two late touchdown passes to make a game of it. They were not enough, and the Browns' loss set up a win-or-you're-out 16th game against Houston.

Strock's south Florida tan was still evident when he took the field in Cleveland Municipal Stadium in a December snowstorm and minus eight-degree wind chill. In the first half, he was intercepted three times and lost a fumble to put the Browns in a 23-7 hole.

Then the guile of a 16-year NFL veteran took over. Strock led three touchdown drives in the second half for a 28-23 win. It set up a rematch with the Oilers in the playoffs.

Completing the theme of the season, Strock was knocked out in the second quarter when he bruised a wrist trying to recover his own fumble. Pagel, by now recovered from his injury, finished the game and the Browns lost, 24-23.

Strock played one more season in Indianapolis before retiring—this time for good.

GERALD MCNEIL

Longtime Browns publicist Dino Lucarelli remembers it as his most embarrassing moment.

At the 1986 training camp at Lakeland Community College, Lucarelli was approached by a short and skinny young man in a Browns T-shirt who asked for complimentary tickets to an upcoming exhibition game.

"I'm sorry," Lucarelli told him. "I can only get tickets for players."

"I am a player," the young man protested. "I'm Gerald McNeil."

Years later, Lucarelli confessed, "I thought he was a ball boy."

Who could blame him? McNeil, who joined the Browns in August after the United States Football League folded, reported to his first NFL camp weighing 122 pounds, he says now. The Browns listed him as 140. He was 5'7".

"The heaviest I weighed with the Browns was 137," McNeil said. "I think I was the lightest player ever in the NFL."

The kick return specialist immediately dazzled teammates with his quickness and slippery elusiveness.

Early on in his first camp, McNeil was having lunch with punter Jeff Gossett, who had competed against him in the USFL. Gossett predicted McNeil would become a fan favorite in Cleveland because of his style and size. He thought McNeil was ripe for a nickname.

As Gossett fingered a tiny ice cube on a lunch tray, he said, "That's it. You're just like an ice cube—cool, tiny, slippery. You're the Cube."

The nickname caught on instantly. Gossett also was right about his prediction. McNeil's popularity soared when fans saw the fearless little returner eluding giants on punts and kickoffs. In his fourth game, McNeil returned a punt 84 yards for a touchdown.

The next week, McNeil played a huge role in the Browns' biggest victory in decades. They won, 27-24, in Pittsburgh's Three Rivers Stadium for the first time after 16 consecutive losses.

McNeil returned a kickoff 100 yards for a touchdown in the second quarter. He remembers being inspired by special teams coach Bill Cowher, who lectured him after a fumbled punt was converted into a Pittsburgh touchdown.

"We're in a TV timeout and he's in my face," McNeil said of the future Steelers head coach. "He's spitting a lot. And he's yelling, 'I'm sending you back out there. We're relying on you. We're going to win this game. Do you hear me?'

"It was the most unbelievable speech ever. Every time I see him I say there is no doubt why he is as good as he is and why people play for him."

McNeil did not have another touchdown return after his first season. But he still holds franchise records with 161 punt returns for 1,545 yards. It was also quite an accomplishment for him to escape major injury in his four seasons.

He wasn't as lucky when he moved on to Houston. In a 1992 preseason game, he took a helmet to his leg and suffered a torn quadriceps muscle. He retired shortly afterwards.

"You get to thinking, 'Man, a little guy like me can get hurt out there,'" McNeil said.

BRIAN BRENNAN

Almost 20 years later, Brian Brennan remembers everything about the play. And why not?

It should have been the play that launched the Browns to their first Super Bowl appearance. It should have given the Browns the psychological edge in two future AFC championship game matchups against the Denver Broncos.

It should have permanently enshrined Brennan in the memory banks of a whole generation of Browns fans.

"It was called 'Two flip wide, Y option, X smash,'" Brennan said. "Reggie Langhorne runs an option on the right side, Webster Slaughter on the left runs a smash route, which leaves me one on one with the safety Dennis Smith, and I'm going to run a corner route. And any time either me or Langhorne are matched up on a safety, Bernie Kosar's going to look for us because typically we beat them.

"So I got to the line, Bernie kind of looked at me with a nod and I'm thinking, 'Yessir, here we go.' They blitz, and it's me one on one with Dennis Smith. I run a very good route, Bernie throws a very poor pass, underthrown, and I slowed down for the ball and make the catch. Dennis Smith misplays it and falls down."

Cleveland Stadium is rocking with 79,915 fans, delighting in the realization of the Browns heading for the Super Bowl in Pasadena, California.

Brennan has the ball in his hands at the Denver 20-yard line. Looking at Smith on the ground, Brennan fakes left and fakes right.

"I didn't know which way to go," Brennan recalled, laughing. "I go back and forth a couple times. He's on the ground and I'm thinking, 'Which way do I go?' I was a little disoriented."

Brennan made it to the end zone to complete the 48-yard play, and the extra point gave the Browns a 20-13 lead with five minutes, 43 seconds to go. The former favorite receiver of Doug Flutie at Boston College finally had the spotlight to himself.

"It was a great feeling," Brennan said. "I was still young [24] in my career. It was a chance for me to shine without Doug Flutie. I was shaking afterwards. I thought I had made the catch to put us in the Super Bowl."

The ensuing Browns kickoff was muffed by Ken Bell, another former Boston College teammate of Brennan's. Bell was buried inside the two-yard line. The crowd's roar reached a new pitch. Ninety-eight yards to Pasadena. Ninety-eight yards to the Super Bowl.

"Then, much to my chagrin, we go into the *prevent defense*," Brennan said, emphasizing the words with derision. "And I watch John Elway throw 10-yard pass after 20-yard pass in no time flat. It was very disappointing to watch. My excitement and elation turned into disbelief."

Elway rode "the Drive" to the Pro Football Hall of Fame. It was the defining moment of his career, more so than his two Super Bowl victories at the end.

Brennan had many more big catches in his Browns career—including two in the end zone in the 1989 AFC championship game in Denver. But he was never in position again to be the city's hero. Elway beat the Browns three times with the Super Bowl on the line.

"We took great pride as an offensive team back then," Brennan said. "The Three Amigos [the nickname given Elway's receivers] couldn't stand up to what our talent was. We had such great confidence and a great chemistry with Bernie. We felt we could score every play.

"We really thought we could beat anybody. But there isn't any team as lucky as Denver."

REGGIE LANGHORNE

One of the strengths of the Browns' division championship teams in the late 1980s was team camaraderie. At the heart of the close-knit group was receiver Reggie Langhorne.

A seventh-round draft choice from unknown Elizabeth City State in 1985, Langhorne was part of a nucleus of young players who grew together and experienced five playoff seasons in a row.

Langhorne, Webster Slaughter and Brian Brennan formed a formidable trio of receivers for quarterback Bernie Kosar.

"Web was the toughest rookie you'd see," Langhorne said. "In his first minicamp, he was running first team with the rookies. Then when the veterans got there, Web actually got in the huddle with the starting lineup and wouldn't be moved. He pretty much said, 'I've been here all week. I'm not leaving.' That's a dude I wanted to hang out with. He was always feisty and confident.

"Brennan, being a white guy playing in the slot, supposedly slow, but the guy never dropped balls. He was always open and had the character of a lion. He looked like a little leprechaun, but he was as tough as anybody you'd play ball with."

Langhorne was the most physical of the three, 6'2" and 195 pounds. And tough. He played the first game of the 1990 season 18 days after having an emergency appendectomy.

But when the Browns made a coaching change in 1991 and brought in Bill Belichick, the playoff run was over. Belichick felt he had to weed out those he considered to be declining players. Langhorne was one of the first popular players Belichick chose to mess with.

The two first clashed when Langhorne missed time in training camp in a contract dispute. Belichick was intent on developing a rookie draft pick named Michael Jackson and played hardball with Langhorne.

"As it got closer to the season, he started taking $10,000 off the table every day, and I couldn't afford it," Langhorne recalled. "I sucked it up and came in. When I got there, we had to run these gassers [40-yard sprints] over and back in so many seconds with your shoulder pads on. The other guys did it with just shorts on. He made me and Michael Dean Perry, who came in the same day, do it with pads on.

"Michael Dean never finished. I did all mine in time. But I weighed 202 pounds. He wanted me to weigh 201, so he fined me every day for that. Every little thing he could do to piss me off, he did."

Langhorne played sparingly until an injury to Brennan forced him into a large role in the third game. He caught passes on three straight plays to set up a field goal in the last seconds that defeated Cincinnati, 14-13.

"We start practice the next week, and Belichick pushed me back to fourth team," Langhorne said. "And he tells me to run scout team. So I got a little frustrated and I said, 'I'm sorry, sir, I'm not going to do that.'"

Langhorne was fined $15,000. He met with Ernie Accorsi, director of football operations, and asked to be traded. When news of the meeting was reported the next day, Belichick suspended Langhorne for conduct detrimental to the team and did not take him to the next game against the New York Giants. That action cost him a $30,000 game check.

After the season, Langhorne left the Browns for the Indianapolis Colts in free agency. It was a sad way for his Browns career to end. But he would get the last laughs.

The Browns played the Colts in the next season's opener. Langhorne caught a touchdown pass in a 14-3 Indianapolis win. To celebrate, he threw the ball in the direction of Belichick.

"Shortly after that, my agent found out that Michael Dean Perry walked out of practice in training camp that year and was only fined $200," Langhorne said. "So we took my fine to arbitration. I wound up getting $44,800 in back pay for when Belichick suspended me."

And Langhorne's Colts played the Browns again, and beat them again, 23-10.

"I went into the offensive and defensive meetings and told them everything about every player and coach," Langhorne said. "I really did not want to lose to [Belichick]."

Langhorne led the Colts in receptions in both of his years with them. In 1993—what proved to be his last NFL season—he had 85 receptions for 1,038 yards. They were career highs for him.

WEBSTER SLAUGHTER

No receiver in Browns history had quite the colorful year that Webster Slaughter enjoyed in 1989.

Besides his record 1,236 receiving yards, Slaughter took on the role of team stylist. He wore specialized orange wristbands and then spiced up his game-day outfit by spray-painting his football shoes orange.

Teammate Eric Metcalf asked him to paint his shoes for a nationally televised Monday night game against the Chicago Bears.

The orange shoes worked like magic.

Slaughter hooked up with Bernie Kosar for a *Monday Night Football*-record 97-yard touchdown play and 186 receiving yards. And Metcalf ran for a touchdown and caught one. The 27-7 Browns win broke a two-game losing streak.

"Then everybody on offense wanted their shoes painted orange," Slaughter said.

As the playoffs approached, the NFL office notified the Browns that either everybody wore orange shoes, or nobody wore them. So the team voted to wear orange shoes for the AFC championship game in Denver.

Slaughter was elected to paint them all. After practice the day before the game, Slaughter spent hours spray-painting his teammates' shoes in the visitor's locker room of Mile High Stadium.

"That gave me a big headache," Slaughter said 14 years later. "The fumes really bothered me. In fact, I have a big picture at my mom's house with me with a towel over my face painting the shoes."

The colorful footwear didn't change the Browns' luck in Denver. They lost, 37-21, as the Broncos swept to their third AFC title in four years. Each time they defeated the Browns.

"Every game we played them I thought we'd win," Slaughter said. "I sure didn't think they could beat us three times in a row."

Slaughter had an unwitting hand in the previous AFC championship loss in Denver following the 1987 season.

His four-yard touchdown catch tied the game, 31-31, with more than 10 minutes to go. After Denver regained the lead with another touchdown, the Browns were driving to tie it for the third time. But Earnest Byner fumbled and cornerback Jeremiah Castille recovered at the three with 65 seconds to play.

"Like the rest of us, Slaughter thought Byner was scoring and he turned and watched," said Ernie Accorsi, director of football operations. "The tackle's the thing that always annoyed me the most because Castille didn't even hit him. He just reached around him and he lost the ball."

In later years, Lindy Infante, the offensive coordinator at the time, said that Slaughter lollygagged on the play and kept Castille in position to make the play.

Slaughter denies it.

"What I do remember is the play was supposed to go inside," he said. "My responsibility was never Jeremiah Castille. It was the safety. So I went inside to get the safety and I sensed the play not coming up inside by his reaction.

"That's when I took Castille and Earnest popped all the way outside of me even. He just didn't hold on to the ball. I thought he had a touchdown, to be honest with you, and then I saw everybody panicking and like everybody else I just started looking around."

Unfortunately for Slaughter, heartbreak endings followed him when he left the Browns.

He was on the Houston Oilers team that blew a 35-3 lead to Buffalo in the 1992 AFC playoffs. He was on the Kansas City Chiefs in 1995 when kicker Lin Elliott missed three field goals in a 10-7 loss to Indianapolis in the playoffs.

BUD CARSON

The Browns were obsessed with defeating Denver Broncos quarterback John Elway in the late 1980s. After successive heartbreaking losses to him in the AFC championship game, most every move the Browns made was with Elway in mind.

That is how Bud Carson came to be their head coach in 1989.

Carson had a distinguished career as a defensive coordinator, first as the architect of the famed "Steel Curtain" defense of the Pittsburgh Steelers and then with the Los Angeles Rams and New York Jets.

At 58, he thought the opportunity to be an NFL head coach had passed him by. That's why he was willing to accept the Browns job with strings attached.

Carson had to accept young Marc Trestman as his offensive coordinator. Trestman was considered a rising head coach candidate by the Browns and had been promoted to coordinator two weeks before Carson was hired. Carson also accepted having virtually no voice in the draft.

Carson seemed to wear those conditions on his sleeve, as if he were doomed to be an ex-coach.

"He always thought he was going to be fired," said Ernie Accorsi, who hired Carson.

That was no more evident than on the day of Carson's surreal debut as head coach. In an emotion-wracked encounter against his friend, Chuck Noll, Carson's defense racked up seven sacks, forced eight turnovers and scored three touchdowns in a record-shattering 51-0 defeat of the Steelers in Pittsburgh.

It was the greatest debut for an NFL head coach and the worst defeat ever suffered by the Steelers.

After the game, Carson looked like he'd been in a streetfight. His white hair was askew and his face was red.

"What can you do after that, huh?" Carson recalled more than 10 years later. "I didn't do anything after that. Like Art Modell said later on, 'That was a fluke.' It sure was.

"I haven't been able to enjoy it with anyone, really. I have the newspaper article of the game framed. Chuck, to this day, is a good friend of mine."

Carson's self-loathing bothered the front office. So did his frankness and openness with the media. But after some in-season growing pains, the plan was being realized.

The Browns defeated Elway in a game in Cleveland in the fourth week and went on to win their division. A heart-pounding triumph over the Buffalo Bills in the playoffs set up a third meeting with Elway in the AFC championship game.

"Bud was the most brilliant defensive coach I've ever been around," Accorsi said. "I love Bud. The problem with him as a head coach is you lose a lot of his value as defensive coordinator.

"We knew we were running out of time with that team. I think he had played him only twice before, but he'd never lost to Elway. I felt if he could just win that game, hiring him would be worth it.

"On the day of the Denver game, I said, 'This is what we brought him in for.'"

Alas, Elway did it to the Browns again. Carson devised a scheme of relentless blitzing. Elway beat it all day. He threw for 385 yards and three touchdowns in a 37-21 Denver victory.

That was the beginning of the end for Carson. His second season was disrupted when eight key veteran players had contract disputes. Although Carson scored another victory over Pittsburgh in the first game, the season quickly disintegrated with three successive losses by progressively larger margins.

"I didn't know how to play the game," Carson said of the politics inherent in the job as Browns head coach.

Carson's last weeks on the job were rife with tension spurred by almost daily reports of his imminent firing. He had one last victory in his bag, however.

It came, ironically, in Denver in a suspenseful Monday night game that was hyped as a "win-or-be-fired" game for him. The Browns won on a last-second field goal.

He was fired four weeks later.

Carson returned to the defensive coordinator ranks with the Jets and St. Louis Rams before retiring in 1997 because of emphysema and asthma.

CHAPTER 5

The 1990s

FELIX WRIGHT

The 1990 preseason was a tumultuous time when the Browns played hardball with eight veteran players seeking new contracts.

Safety Felix Wright was one of the holdouts. At the time, owner Art Modell was trying to break in son David, then 26, into a more meaningful role with the club. His first major assignment was to negotiate a contract with Wright.

It led to an embarrassing public confrontation prior to the team's first exhibition game at home.

Wright had consistently improved in each of his first five seasons with the Browns. The previous year was his best yet. He led the NFL with nine interceptions and was third on the defense in tackles. Yet the Browns were offering only a nominal raise, and Wright joined six other teammates in holding out.

Wright's brother, Charles, had been signed as a cornerback prospect and already was in camp. Felix's holdout did not change the plans of his parents to attend the season's first exhibition game.

After sending his parents to their seats, Wright stopped to drop off a ticket for teammate Frank Minnifield at the Stadium will call window. On the way out, he bumped into David Modell leaving his office.

Modell, smoking a cigar, initiated an animated discussion with Wright about his holdout. It only lasted a minute, but fans recognized both men and stopped to watch the scene.

"We kind of nodded to each other, and then I continued walking," Wright recalled. "He stopped me and said, 'Felix, what are you going to do? When are you going to come in?'

"I said, 'That's why I have an agent—to do my negotiating for me.'

"About that time, people started coming around and watching. And then David Modell said, 'Well, you're not getting a penny more.'

"I said, 'David, I'm not going to stand here and negotiate with you.' Minnifield came by and we went to our seats and the next thing I knew there were four or five television cameras around me at my seat."

The dispute was settled a month later. Wright signed a one-year contract with an option to become a free agent after the season. He moved on to the Minnesota Vikings, but he returned to live in Cleveland after retirement.

David Modell never lived down the incident.

ERIC METCALF

During the height of their playoff knockdowns with the Denver Broncos, the Browns traded with their AFC rivals on draft day in 1989 to acquire the rights to select Eric Metcalf.

The triple offensive threat from Texas, who doubled on the Longhorns' track team as a world-class long jumper, was smaller but faster than his father, Terry, a Pro Bowl return specialist for the St. Louis Cardinals in the 1970s.

"I was obsessed with Metcalf," Ernie Accorsi, director of football operations, said years later. "I don't think we're even in contention in '89 without him. He was one of my favorite players of my career."

Shorter than his listed height of 5'10" and a sturdy 190 pounds, Metcalf could not be stereotyped in the NFL game as a rusher, a receiver, or a return specialist. He was a playmaker.

He first flashed his stop-and-go, cut-on-a-dime cutback ability on a *Monday Night Football* game in Cincinnati in his third NFL appearance. Metcalf caught a short pass and made a couple of hop-and-skip moves that left a Bengals defender clutching air while falling to the ground. Metcalf's first career touchdown, only five yards long, was replayed for days on national television.

"He was one of the most electrifying players I've been around," Accorsi said.

The Browns felt Metcalf was the jolt of youth and energy the aging team needed to lift them to the Super Bowl.

In fact, the rookie led the Browns in 1989 in rushing and touchdowns. And then he returned a kickoff 90 yards for a touchdown in a playoff win over Buffalo—the first postseason scoring return in club history.

Alas, the Browns were tripped up in the AFC championship game by Denver for the third time in four years.

The playoff team was broken up, but Metcalf stayed on through 1994 and provided many more jaw-dropping performances.

He cites as his most memorable day a 1992 game in Los Angeles against the Raiders, in which he scored four touchdowns—three on receptions.

"The thing I remember most about that game wasn't on the field," Metcalf said. "When I was a kid, I just loved Magic Johnson to death. And still do. And he was at that game.

"And at halftime I walked right by him and I wanted to talk to him. I thought, 'No, I'm in the middle of this game. I'll get him later.' But he was gone after that. That sticks out in my mind, that my all-time favorite basketball player got to see one of my best games."

In 1993, Metcalf almost single-handedly led a victory over the Pittsburgh Steelers with punt returns for touchdowns of 91 and 75 yards—the longest pair of scoring returns in an NFL game at the time.

"I thought I would be on the *Sports Illustrated* cover after that," Metcalf recalled, "but then Joe Carter had to go ahead and hit that [winning] home run in the World Series [for the Toronto Blue Jays]. That was my first and only chance to be on the cover."

A week later, coach Bill Belichick shook up his team and the city by releasing quarterback Bernie Kosar with the Browns in first place. They would lose six of their next eight games.

"That was like leaving us to die, with no chance to succeed," Metcalf said.

Metcalf finished his Browns career with a franchise-record seven return touchdowns, plus another in the playoffs. He added five more playing with six other teams. His 12 return touchdowns in his NFL career are second on the all-time list.

"People maybe wouldn't believe this, but I tell my wife all the time that I want to be in the Browns hall of fame," Metcalf said. "There are so many great players who played for that team and did great things. Everybody knows about them. If I'm considered one of the greatest Browns, then I'd feel I've done a lot."

Metcalf said that at some point in his Browns career, he longed to move to greener pastures. After playing for six other teams, he learned the old adage.

"You find out the grass isn't greener on the other side," Metcalf said. "I always tell people now there's no place I'd rather play than Cleveland. If I could play there forever, I would.

"Just because of the tradition, the fans, the love people have for you as a Cleveland Brown. When I went to other teams, it just didn't feel the same."

BILL BELICHICK

No coach in Browns history was excoriated as severely in the media and by the fans as Bill Belichick.

Through a myriad of circumstances—some in Belichick's control, and others out of his control—the five years beginning in 1991 and ending with owner Art Modell moving his team to Baltimore are considered the darkest period of the old Browns.

Belichick was the league's hottest head coach candidate after he coordinated the New York Giants defense to a Super Bowl victory over the high-scoring Buffalo Bills. His discipline and no-nonsense approach were seen by Modell as necessary qualities to steer the Browns through a painful transition period.

"There were a lot of great Cleveland players when I got there who were at the end of their careers," Belichick recalled. "Whether I released them and they never played again, or they played marginally for a year or two afterwards, there was a long list of them."

Early on, Belichick had several run-ins with popular players. An increasing backlash from fans obscured the fact that his teams were getting better.

But his release of quarterback Bernie Kosar in the middle of his third season was a *cause celebre* that polarized the market and launched a lynch mob mentality.

Kosar was a community icon who presided over the team's five-year playoff run in the late 1980s. He and the coach disagreed about play calling and style of offense, and about Kosar's skills. Their relationship eroded to the point that one often defied the other during games.

When it descended to where they could no longer coexist, Modell sided with Belichick. He agreed to release Kosar in the middle of the 1993 season because of "his diminishing skills." At the time, the team was tied for first place with a 5-3 record, and backup quarterback Vinny Testaverde was sidelined with a separated shoulder.

"The only thing I can say is I did what I thought was best at the time," Belichick said 10 years later. "If things had been different, who knows? Nobody has more respect for Bernie Kosar as a football player, for his preparation, for his love of football and for his intelligence than I do.

"In the end, I thought Vinny was a good quarterback. We know the decision. Could it have been handled differently? Sure it could have. Better? Maybe, I don't know. It was an emotional thing, and I'm sure those emotions would have flowed no matter what would have happened."

The Browns lost six of their last eight games to finish 7-9. Loud, vicious chants of "Bill must go" filled Cleveland Municipal Stadium every game.

Modell defiantly dug in behind his unpopular coach and announced after the season, "I am so sure about Bill Belichick

Bill Belichick (r) with Bernie Kosar (© Brockway Sports Photos)

that if I am wrong about him, I will leave Cleveland and the game of football. He is the last coach I hire as coach of the Browns."

The following year, the Browns went to the playoffs with an 11-5 record and set a franchise record for fewest points allowed in a 16-game schedule.

"That '94 defense that gave up 204 points was one of the better defenses in the history of the NFL," Belichick said.

Unbeknownst to the public, Modell was having financial problems and careening toward bankruptcy.

The Browns started the 1995 season with a 3-1 record when rumors surfaced that Modell was contemplating the unfathomable—moving the team to Baltimore to save himself from personal bankruptcy. The team slumped to 4-4 before the rumors turned to fact and Modell made the announcement that shattered the city.

"The situation really deteriorated within the team," Belichick said. "I could see where it was going. From the first night forward [after the Houston game following the announcement], I thought my chances of being with the Browns for the '96 season were not very good."

The Browns lost all remaining games except one—the final home game against Cincinnati. Modell fired Belichick in a phone call shortly after that game.

Belichick revived his career as an assistant coach, and then was named head coach of the New England Patriots in 2000. The following year, he coached them to an improbable Super Bowl championship. They repeated as champions in 2003.

Despite the abuse and grief he took from fans and media in Cleveland, Belichick never held it against them.

"Football was so important to everybody in that area," he said. "All the interest and the knowledge the fans had for the game was special. To be part of that was breathtaking. It was an overwhelming feeling."

ERIC TURNER

The Browns were consumed with defense in 1991. Bill Belichick, the hottest defensive assistant coach in the NFL, was hired as head coach. He used his first draft pick, the league's second overall, on Eric Turner, a safety from UCLA.

Turner had the striking good looks of a Hollywood movie star. He arrived with gold jewelry and a bright smile and a nickname—E-rock—that foretold his hard-hitting playing style.

"Obviously, I love to hit people," he said. "That's the nature of the game. And whenever I make a hit on somebody, I want to make sure they know I'm out there."

The first tackle he made in his first game bent the facemask of Cincinnati Bengals running back James Brooks. In his first start, he intercepted the second pass of the game and returned it 42 yards for a touchdown. In his second start, he forced two fumbles.

In his fourth season, Turner had one of the best years of any Browns safety. He tied for the league lead with nine interceptions as Belichick's defense carried the team to the playoffs. In what would be the last playoff game in old Cleveland Municipal Stadium, Turner added another interception in a victory over the New England Patriots.

"He was as good a defensive player as there was that year," said Scott Pioli, a Browns scout at the time. "He did things that changed the course of games."

The defining moment of that season occurred in Texas Stadium in the 14th game against the Dallas Cowboys, who had won the previous two Super Bowls. On the last play of the game, Turner tackled Cowboys tight end Jay Novacek at the goal line as time ran out to preserve a 19-14 victory.

The 1994 season was as good as it got for Turner.

He fractured a bone in his lower back the following year. The team fell apart after owner Art Modell disclosed plans to move the franchise to Baltimore.

Weeks later, Cleveland city officials organized a bus trip for fans to demonstrate their anger in front of the ABC's *Monday Night Football* cameras at a Browns game in Pittsburgh.

The night before at the team hotel, Turner was wheeled into a team meeting on a hospital bed.

"Things were unraveling on the team," Belichick said. "When he came from the hospital to talk to the team, I'm telling you it was impressive."

Turner spent one year in Baltimore with his unhappy teammates, and then realized a career dream by joining the Los Angeles Raiders.

At the age of 31, Turner was felled by abdominal cancer while still an active player. A supremely private person, he issued a press release in 2000 to dispute reports he was gravely ill. Two weeks later, he died.

Not even his best friend with the Browns, Eric Metcalf, knew how ill Turner was.

"The last time we talked, we were going to meet in Las Vegas after the '99 season and he told me he was having problems with his stomach, but he never told me exactly what they were," Metcalf said. "So we never got to see each other again. When I found out what was wrong, it was too late."

At the time of Turner's death, former teammate Rob Burnett said, "What a good guy. He was well raised, knew how to handle himself, well spoken. When you think of role models, outstanding athletes, that would be Eric Turner. He didn't even curse. He's what you would want your son or grandson to grow up to be."

Tom Tupa

He played quarterback at Ohio State and was good enough to be chosen in the third round of the NFL draft in 1988. But the best thing to happen to Tom Tupa was a switch to full-time punter in his second season with the Browns in 1994.

He went on to punt nine more years with three teams. Tupa punted in two Super Bowls, winning the championship after the 2002 season with the Tampa Bay Buccaneers.

"When I was released in 1992 as a quarterback [from the Indianapolis Colts], I thought I was done then," Tupa said. "I've been lucky."

The native of Brecksville, Ohio, entered the record books in the 1994 season when he became the first NFL player to score a two-point conversion. The league had instituted the two-point option after touchdowns that spring.

The Browns capitalized on the new rule in their first game. After their first touchdown of the season, Tupa lined up in his usual spot as holder on placekicks. Instead of spotting the ball, however, Tupa sprang up and ran it in for a two-point conversion.

He would score similarly on two other occasions to tie for the league lead that season and earn the nickname "Two-Point Tommy."

Steve Everitt

Teammates avoided the locker of Steve Everitt, a center who was taken with the Browns' first-round draft choice in 1993.

A fan of heavy metal music and pro wrestling, the unkempt Everitt was known for wearing the same clothes every day—torn white T-shirt, tan camouflage pants and basketball shoes with no socks.

"He'd wear the same clothes two weeks in a row," said coach Bill Belichick. "He didn't clean out his locker twice a season. One day, one of the linemen bought a fish at a market and put it in his locker. The first day, he didn't notice. The second day, something smelled and he figured it was just his locker. The third day, he finally climbed in and took it out."

One time, a club official entered the players' lounge area and saw Everitt leaning against a dining table and stuffing barbecued ribs in a gym bag.

"You don't have to do that," the club official said. "Just put them in a paper bag and take them home."

"I can fit more in here," Everitt responded.

When Art Modell moved his club to Baltimore in 1996 and renamed it the Ravens, Everitt was one of the team's unhappiest players. Although a native of Miami, he played at Michigan and loved the Midwest. He hated leaving Cleveland.

Everitt honored the memory of the Browns by displaying a Browns cap in his grungy locker in Baltimore.

The team's first exhibition game in Baltimore was televised nationally. At one point, cameras focused on Everitt on the sideline. He had removed his helmet. On his head he wore a Browns bandanna. It was his way of saying hello to friends and fans in Cleveland.

The Ravens fined Everitt $5,000. He said it was worth it.

TODD PHILCOX

Coach Bill Belichick stunned everyone in the middle of the 1993 season when he released popular quarterback Bernie Kosar with the Browns tied for first place with a 5-3 record.

Compounding the shock was the fact that Vinny Testaverde, Kosar's top backup, was out with a separated shoulder at the time.

This monumental oversight thrust third-stringer Todd Philcox into the limelight as Kosar's immediate successor. Philcox had started only one game in three previous NFL seasons.

The results were sadly predictable. Philcox's debut in Seattle against the Seahawks was a disaster.

On his first play, Philcox was sacked and lost a fumble. The game went downhill from there. The Browns committed seven turnovers and lost, 22-5. In all, Philcox lost two fumbles and threw two interceptions. He completed nine of 20 passes for 85 yards—and 50 of the yards came on one completion.

Philcox threw four interceptions in his next start, another loss. He was better in his third start, but the Browns lost again. He built a lead in his fourth start before being permanently replaced by Testaverde.

Philcox became a sympathetic figure. His plight inspired *Plain Dealer* columnist Dick Feagler to invent the word "philcoxed."

Feagler wrote: "Phil-coxed ... (adjective) ... to be put into an absolutely no-win situation because of the stupidity, madness or miscalculations of one's superiors."

Philcox was released after the season. He subsequently was signed by San Diego, Tampa Bay and New England before retiring after the 1999 season.

Years later, Belichick offered this summation of Philcox: "Good guy. Was put in a tough spot."

ANDRE RISON

No player better epitomized the final dismal year of the old Browns in Cleveland than Andre Rison.

After losing to the Pittsburgh Steelers in a playoff game in 1994, owner Art Modell sought to make a splashy acquisition to keep fans interested and pump up a sagging offense. His football people chose to pursue Rison, a receiver who averaged 80 catches a year in the run-and-shoot offense of the Atlanta Falcons.

Rison also had a celebrity fiancee—a singer in a rap group named Lisa (Left Eye) Lopes. She gained a degree of infamy by torching Rison's home in a domestic dispute before he joined the Browns.

At the annual NFL meetings in March, Modell disclosed to national writers how much he prized Rison.

"He's the biggest star we've signed," Modell said. "He's the first home run hitter we've had in a long time. He is truly a potential Hall of Famer. Since Jim Brown, Leroy Kelly and Paul Warfield, we have not had the caliber of player offensively like Andre Rison."

The only problem was Rison had not signed a contract yet. Modell's raves inspired Rison's agent to raise his client's price tag. Instead of a $1 million cash signing bonus, which was the range the two sides originally discussed, Rison now demanded $5 million. The overall contract was for $17 million for five years.

Because Modell had hyped Rison's signing so heavily to his fans, he felt internal pressure to agree to the inflated contract.

Modell later said he had to take out a loan in his wife's name to pay the signing bonus. He used it as evidence of not being able to compete with other NFL owners when he pleaded his case to move his team to Baltimore.

Several years later, coach Bill Belichick said the inflated contract affected Rison's play.

"When he got the money, he had such an attitude about doing it his way," Belichick said. "Then when things got bad, he threw in the towel even more. Giving him all that money up front was a license to him that 'Andre, you're the man. Just do what you've been doing. Why change anything?' That's the way he approached the game."

Rison had a tumultuous season in Cleveland. He alienated fans early on when he defended Modell's move to Baltimore. He skipped team meetings, tanked it on the field, practiced touchdown celebrations instead of pass routes, feuded with the starting quarterback, made obscene gestures to the home crowd and blasted fans for booing him.

He finished with a career-low 47 catches and three touchdowns.

When the team moved to Baltimore, Rison was released by Modell.

"I've been places where loyalty was not shown before and where there was a lot of cutthroat negotiations, but this came from a man I had respect for, and it shook me up for a minute," Rison said.

CHAPTER 6

The New Browns, 1999 and Beyond

AL LERNER

At his funeral in October of 2002, Al Lerner was eulogized as a marine, patriot, loving father and doting grandfather, enormously successful businessman with rare intellect and uncanny street smarts, and generous philanthropist.

There wasn't a single mention of the role of Browns owner that connected him with the average sports fan in Cleveland.

Owning the Browns was a miniscule portion of Lerner's life accomplishments. But his last years were devoted to restoring pro football in Cleveland and developing the expansion franchise into a first-class organization.

"It was a way that he could continue to grow his investment in Cleveland," said son Randy Lerner, who took over ownership after his father's death. "The guy was a sports fan his whole life and was an athlete as a young guy.

"He had reached, I think, a stage in life where his desire to continue to give was growing and the absolute purest form of

Al Lerner (AP/WWP)

giving, which was to just make donations, started to expand to things like this."

Lerner outbid a field of six ownership groups for the Browns' expansion franchise in September of 1998. His bid of $530 million was a record at the time for a professional sports franchise. He later spent more than $12 million in renovations to Cleveland Browns Stadium.

Until he joined the effort of Mayor Michael White to bring a new team to Cleveland, Lerner was criticized for his role in helping Art Modell move the old Browns to Baltimore. Lerner and Modell were friends and business partners since the mid-1980s.

When Modell's financial problems intensified in the mid-1990s, Lerner introduced him to influential contacts in Maryland. Modell actually signed the contract to move his team to Baltimore in Lerner's corporate jet parked at Baltimore-Washington International Airport in July of 1995.

Lerner explained his involvement as helping a friend on the verge of bankruptcy.

"Was I involved? Yeah, I was," he said. "Was it for the right reasons? I thought so. I don't feel guilty. I feel stupid, but I don't feel guilty."

Behind the scenes, Lerner worked with White and the NFL to bring a team back to Cleveland and have a new stadium built. He kept a low profile and insisted he was not a candidate to own the team. He changed his mind when Carmen Policy resigned as president of the San Francisco 49ers and joined Lerner in a partnership of two.

"I just thought it was critical for this city to not have that gaping hole on the lake and not have a football team, so that's why I got involved," he explained.

As owner, Lerner lavished his players with amenities such as gourmet meals year-round, valet parking service on game days, private parties for families and the best facilities that money could buy.

Lerner had a net worth estimated of at least $4.7 billion, yet he mingled easily with players and spoke to the team often about his passion to win and his experiences as a marine fighter pilot. He embraced players from humble backgrounds.

"He closed that gap for one reason; because he wasn't born with a silver spoon in his mouth," said cornerback Corey Fuller.

The only son of Russian immigrants, Lerner was born in Brooklyn, N.Y., and grew up in the back of his family's luncheonette in Queens. A former furniture salesman, his business career started when he invested in apartment buildings and other commercial real estate. He moved to Shaker Heights in 1960 and made it his home for the rest of his life.

In 1991, Lerner rescued a money-losing bank and eventually took its fledgling credit card operation public. MBNA Corp. would become the nation's largest independent bank lender through credit cards.

As his wealth grew, Lerner and wife Norma gave more than $125 million to Cleveland health care institutions, the Cleveland Clinic and University Hospitals.

A year before his death caused by brain cancer, Lerner said, "I'm never going to be in the Pro Bowl. I'm not going to win an Oscar, not going to be in the Canton Hall of Fame. So the closest I'm going to get to is having done pretty well and being able to convert that into a legacy, which in my case I hope to be in the field of medicine, where I can have some contribution to where people will get treated better or be less sick, and people who develop diseases will get better research.

"That's what I hope my legacy's going to be, not just that I made a bunch of money."

CARMEN POLICY

For months during discussions of a new Cleveland Browns expansion franchise, Cleveland billionaire financier Al Lerner publicly insisted he would not be a candidate to own the team.

So why did he not only declare his candidacy in July of 1998, but ultimately outbid five other groups and buy the Browns for $530 million, which was then a record for a professional sports franchise?

"The only thing that could have possibly gotten me involved in this thing was Carmen Policy," Lerner said in 1998. "The idea of having the shot at creating the kind of organization that Carmen can create … that is irresistible."

Policy grew up in the same rough Youngstown neighborhood as former billionaire developer Edward J. DeBartolo. He graduated from Youngstown State University and Georgetown University Law Center and settled down as a practicing lawyer. His clients ranged from major corporations to irreputable figures in the Mahoning Valley organized crime world.

In 1979, Policy joined the 49ers as legal counsel. His first official task was to negotiate the contract of new coach Bill Walsh. As Walsh built the 49ers into an NFL powerhouse, Policy climbed the corporate ladder and was named chief executive in 1991.

Under DeBartolo's ownership, the 49ers spared no expense in attacking their goal of winning the Super Bowl. By the time Policy resigned, the 49ers had earned five championships.

So it caused great fanfare when Policy was introduced as Lerner's partner in ownership of the Browns. He received a 10 percent equity stake and the position of chief executive and president.

Cleveland mayor Michael R. White anointed him "the Yoda of football" and thanked him for returning to Northeast Ohio to head the new Browns.

"I have no doubt, without putting pressure on him, that one day in our lifetime, this team is going to go to the Super Bowl under his leadership," White predicted.

Policy pledged to build a "first-class, winning franchise … it will be reflective of what this community wants and deserves."

"For someone from the neighborhood in Youngstown where I grew up, coming through the ranks the way I did, to be sitting here hearing a man of Al Lerner's stature call me partner, suggesting that he has enough faith in me to take a cherished, treasured institution like the Browns and be given the role of creating the organization … it's phenomenal," Policy said.

Shortly after Lerner's organization took hold, Policy warned, "Hang on tight. We're going to be pressing the envelope."

Within a month on the job, the Browns were assessed their first league fine, of $10,000, for "tampering" with former 49ers assistant coach Mike Holmgren, who was contemplating leaving as coach of the Green Bay Packers. Policy's crime was in saying at a public luncheon that Holmgren would make a fine coach of the Browns.

Building the "bricks and mortar" of the new Browns franchise in a uniquely compressed timeline mandated by the NFL was a task few executives could achieve. Policy pulled it off to good reviews. But building the football operation was more problematical.

After two seasons and a 5-27 record, the Browns fired their first coach, Chris Palmer. It was the shortest tenure for any first-time coach of an NFL expansion team. Policy pointedly accepted the responsibility of the dismissal when he made the announcement of the firing with nobody else at his side.

Policy then spearheadeded the relentless recruitment of a successor, Butch Davis, who had spurned several NFL offers in six years as coach at the University of Miami.

Davis instantly turned around the team's fortunes. In his second season—the fourth year of the franchise—Davis coached the new Browns to a 9-7 record and their first appearance in the AFC playoffs.

Lerner did not live to see the team in the playoffs. He died of brain cancer in October of 2002. But he did foresee the turnaround, and he credited Policy for convincing him to not stand pat after those two brutal seasons.

"Let me tell you something about Carmen," Lerner said in 2001. "He knows what [winning] is supposed to feel like. He's very smooth and he knows the right way to handle things, but you don't mess with him. He's got a lot of guts."

After Lerner died, Policy sold back his 10 percent equity in the Browns to the Lerner family. He resigned as president and CEO in April of 2004 to start a winery in Napa Valley, California.

DWIGHT CLARK

Dwight Clark caught the most important pass in San Francisco 49ers history. After retirement, he grabbed hold of Carmen Policy's coattails and pursued a career as a football executive.

When Policy left the 49ers to run the expansion Browns, he tabbed Clark as the new team's general manager. There was no search. No other candidate was even speculated, much less interviewed.

"Carmen is the best at what he does," Browns owner Al Lerner said the day Clark was introduced in Cleveland. "I believe—I know Carmen believes—Dwight Clark is the best at what he does."

The catch Clark made of Joe Montana's pass against the Dallas Cowboys in the 1981 NFC championship game propelled the 49ers to their first Super Bowl. It was immortalized on the cover of *Sports Illustrated* and made him an everlasting football hero.

It also sealed his friendship with Policy and opened doors of opportunity that otherwise would be slammed shut to him.

"It kind of promoted you into a position of notoriety for people in the Bay Area," Clark conceded.

Surely it did not qualify Clark to be Cleveland's general manager. The decisions Clark made charted the important first steps taken by the new franchise.

"This is a once-in-a-lifetime opportunity," he said.

He called on past associations in building the team's first roster. Nine former 49ers participated in the first training camp. They were accustomed to the 49ers' easy-going practice style. Many of them clashed with first coach Chris Palmer, who came from a different school of thought.

Clark was involved in every player acquisition in the first two years. He was 100 percent behind the selections of Tim Couch and Courtney Brown, the "cornerstones" chosen with the Browns' top choices in 1999 and 2000.

There were other draft successes, such as Kevin Johnson, Daylon McCutcheon and Dennis Northcutt. But the clunkers far outnumbered them.

Terms of the expansion deal gave the Browns seven additional selections in each of their first two drafts. Clark eventually utilized 24 of the Browns' 28 picks. By the end of the 2002 season, only seven were still with the team. Most were out of the NFL.

Clark survived the firing of first coach Palmer after the 2000 season, but lasted only one year under Butch Davis, his successor, before he was forced out.

Clark disputed reports he clashed with Davis. In truth, his duties were usurped by Pete Garcia, Davis's "right-hand man" who arrived with him from University of Miami.

In his farewell news conference conducted over the phone, Clark said, "I think a major accomplishment was helping to get the organization up and running in a really short period of time and helping to choose some of the early players. I would say we didn't win a championship. Therefore, there's no great accomplishment."

Clark, who had a year remaining on his original five-year contract, was given a generous termination settlement. He moved to North Carolina and dropped out of the NFL.

CHRIS PALMER

Chris Palmer was the first coach of the expansion Cleveland Browns, but not the first choice.

When team president Carmen Policy and general manager Dwight Clark exhausted a list of candidates with whom they were familiar, Palmer was selected as much for his willingness to plunge into an unwinnable situation as any other qualification.

Palmer was an earnest man who looked more like a sixth-grade history teacher than a football coach. He had a credible history developing quarterbacks as an offensive coordinator, and was interviewed at the same time for vacant head coaching positions with the Kansas City Chiefs and Baltimore Ravens.

But Policy and Clark kept getting the cold shoulder from coaches who considered an expansion team a coaching graveyard. The final insult came from Minnesota Vikings assistant coach Brian Billick, who spurned Clark's in-person overture to join him on a plane to Cleveland because of a scheduled job interview with Baltimore owner Art Modell.

Palmer was offered the job two days later.

It didn't take long for Palmer to realize the enormity of the task at hand.

"I got hired the 21st of January," he recalled. "I tried to put together a coaching staff, and sometime in February, 20 days later, we had the expansion draft. The first year we were on a treadmill, where you just keep going and going."

Palmer received no favor from the league when his first game was scheduled against the rival Pittsburgh Steelers and broadcast nationally in prime time. The Steelers won, 43-0.

The Browns lost seven games before notching their first victory on a Hail Mary touchdown pass as time expired against New Orleans. Their other win that first season came on a last-second field goal in Pittsburgh. It was sweet revenge against the team that spoiled Palmer's coaching debut.

From the outset, Palmer tried to institute discipline and a tough attitude by practicing his players hard. Unfortunately for him, many of them were wooed to Cleveland on the promise of Policy and Clark that the Browns would follow the lax training regimen known to the San Francisco 49ers.

Veteran players rebelled and made Palmer's job even more difficult.

The second year, Palmer's team won two of its first three games before injuries decimated the shallow roster. In the middle of the year, quarterback Tim Couch broke his thumb when a nondescript practice player hit him on the last play of a Thursday practice.

With the team at 2-7, Policy gave Palmer the dreaded vote of confidence and guaranteed "he's our coach, he's going to be our coach … we haven't even considered the fact that wouldn't be here next year."

The Browns won one more game—against former Browns coach Bill Belichick's New England Patriots—before suffering back-to-back losses of 44-7 and 48-0.

The week between those games, Palmer, wearing down under the stress, issued a comment that caused Policy and owner Al Lerner to scratch their heads.

"Sometimes I feel like I'm driving a runaway train," Palmer said.

After the season, Policy and Lerner conducted lengthy review sessions with Palmer and Clark to set a course for correcting the two-year record of 5-27. Policy looked for a new direction out of Palmer. The coach advised, "Stick to the plan."

Palmer thus became the first ex-coach of the new Browns. His two-year tenure was the shortest of any NFL coach with an expansion team.

"All I know is I can look Al Lerner in the face and Carmen Policy in the face and say with what we had, we did the best we could," Palmer said. "And I know my peers feel that way. The people that know in this business see it that way."

Palmer returned to Cleveland in 2002 as offensive coordinator of the Houston Texans, another expansion team.

"When you put your heart and soul into two years of building something, you feel attached," he said prior to his visit. "When I retire, I'm going to be a Cleveland Browns fan. I feel real attached to the city and the team."

ORLANDO BROWN

Orlando Brown's mother nicknamed him Zeus before he was born prematurely weighing three pounds, two ounces.

Her son would become the biggest Cleveland Brown of all time, and the most volatile. Zeus was an apt nickname for someone 6'7" and 375 pounds.

He joined the Browns first in 1993 as a raw offensive lineman from a small black college in South Carolina. He was equally undeveloped in social skills, having grown up in a crime-ridden section of Washington, D.C. He never socialized with white people prior to joining the Browns, he said.

Brown had a temper that coach Bill Belichick immediately plotted to rein in.

Belichick would assign teammates to bait Brown into fighting, and then fine him $1,000 each time he'd take the bait. Eventually, Brown became a good enough player to start in the NFL.

He hit the NFL free agency lottery in 1999 when the new Browns gave him $27 million to return to Cleveland and be a leader on the expansion team. The contract was the biggest ever for an NFL offensive lineman.

The day he returned to Cleveland, Brown slammed a fist on a table and barked, "I'm ready to play ball. I'm ready to bust some heads and I'm ready to get some Ws."

The new Browns liked that fire in his belly. They weren't as familiar with Brown's upbringing as was Belichick. Soon they discovered this was no act.

The Browns won for the first time as an expansion team in their eighth game in New Orleans. They won it on a Hail Mary touchdown pass as time ran out. The next day, game film revealed Brown throwing a hard forearm shiver to the back of New Orleans pass rusher Jared Tomich that knocked him to the turf.

A few days later, Brown received a $5,000 fine for the illegal hit. If a game official had seen it, the winning touchdown would have been nullified.

"I've been doing that since I was in the league," Brown shrugged. "I've always been one of the top dirtiest players in the league."

At this point, coach Chris Palmer privately questioned Brown's state of mind. Brown kept a live goldfish in his locker, on the advice of a team psychologist, to calm him. "He's not right," Palmer said.

The coach denied a female reporter's request to interview Brown one on one because he feared for her safety. Palmer's concerns puzzled reporters because they had always known Brown to be an engaging personality, always polite.

A few weeks later, Palmer's fears were realized.

In a game against the Jacksonville Jaguars, Brown accidentally was hit in the right eye by a penalty flag thrown by referee Jeff Triplette. The impact of the flag, weighted with three ounces of metal BBs, staggered Zeus and angered him.

He fell to one knee and was helped to the sideline by teammates. As the eye puffed up, Brown stormed on the field and shoved the 6'3" Triplette to the ground with both hands. Zeus hovered over Triplette, shrieking and pointing to his right eye, as teammates swooped in and escorted him away.

Brown was ejected from the game. Two security guards and a teammate tried to contain him as he stomped to the locker room, kicking yard markers on the way out.

"I've never seen anything like that," said Jacksonville coach Tom Coughlin. "At first it was disbelief. I was shocked that it had taken place."

Afterward, an ashen-faced Palmer alluded to his private concerns when he said, "I've tried to work with the player and his emotions during the course of the year, and obviously I've failed in that situation."

Initial reactions of outrage toward Brown turned to sympathy when it was disclosed that his father, Claude, was blinded with glaucoma in both eyes. Brown spent six days in the hospital suffering from impaired vision, bleeding and intense pressure in the eye.

He was suspended two games by the NFL, costing him $47,000 in game checks.

Brown never played again for the Browns. He was released the following September after collecting $374,000 in game checks for the 2000 season and qualifying for another year of pension and health benefits.

Six months later, Brown, represented by a law firm bearing the name of O.J. Simpson lead attorney Johnnie Cochran, sued the NFL for $200 million.

"Psychologically, he's devastated," said lawyer Clifford Stern. "He was born and bred to hit on a football field. He has [three] children he expected to see him play in a Pro Bowl. Now he's just a big guy who's a has-been."

In 2002, the NFL reached a settlement with Brown for an estimated $10 million. He returned to play for the Baltimore Ravens the next season.

JIM PYNE

Offensive linemen usually are recognized only for doing something wrong—holding, giving up a sack, false-starting. Jim Pyne changed that on February 9, 1999.

The occasion was the Browns' expansion draft.

To give it the feel of a big event, the NFL spent more than $50,000 to stage the ceremonial roster stocking of the new team in the old Canton Civic Center, a few miles from the Pro Football Hall of Fame. Every NFL team had a representative on hand. ESPN broadcast the proceedings live.

There was not the drama of an NFL college draft, but the anticipation of seeing live players, finally, after a three-year hiatus was enough to excite the 4,000 fans in attendance.

The day before, the Browns secretly invited five players they intended to choose from among the pool of 150 castoffs—overpriced, aging, or injury-riddled players made available to them. But they never told the players who would be the first introduced.

Gene Washington of the NFL office stirred the anticipation when he announced, "The time is now ... and the Browns are on the clock."

Behind a giant curtain, somebody tapped Pyne on the shoulder and said, "Congratulations, you're the first guy."

Pyne, 6'2" and 297 pounds, parted the curtain and strode onstage in a double-breasted, silvery suit. Beneath a shiny, shaved head, Pyne grinned from ear to ear as the audience saluted him. No offensive lineman ever made a grander entrance.

"No one really knows who you are as an offensive lineman," Pyne said years later. "But I will say this, the Cleveland Browns fans are knowledgeable and probably did know who I was."

Pyne, who had played five years with Tampa Bay and Detroit, would start all 16 games at left guard for the first-year Browns. The next season, he blew out his right knee in the second game. Pyne was waived in his third training camp with the Browns after a coaching change.

"Probably the biggest thing I'll remember about my time in Cleveland is meeting my wife there," he said. "It was by far the best place I played—the most fun, with the greatest fans and the greatest people.

"You don't realize what a Browns fan is until you play there. Everybody's got a story about where they were when Red Right 88 happened, or when John Elway did the drive. They live and die with that. So it was an exciting time for me."

DAVE WOHLABAUGH

The first major free agent signed by the Browns when they rejoined the NFL as an expansion team in 1999 was Dave Wohlabaugh. He had been the starting center for the New England Patriots in five playoff games and the 1996 season Super Bowl.

Wohlabaugh was born in Hamburg, N.Y., just a three-hour drive east of Cleveland. He liked the area and the feeling of being part of a franchise building from the ground up. He agreed to a seven-year contract for $26.25 million without visiting any other teams.

"I was very excited," Wohlabaugh said. "There was some unknown, being an expansion team. But nobody thought of losing. We thought we could win."

The Browns were 2-14 and 3-13 the first two seasons.

"The first two years were tough," he said. "As critical as the fans were, the players were more critical of themselves."

A coaching change to Butch Davis in year three turned things around. The Browns went 7-9 and then 9-7 in 2002. They needed to win their 16th game against Atlanta and then sweat out two other NFL games to qualify for the playoffs.

"I think the most memorable game was the Falcons game," Wohlabaugh said of the 24-16 victory that eventually qualified the new Browns for their first postseason appearance. "The fans were unbelievable that game. To me, that was everything that Cleveland Browns football was about when I got there. That was everything I was told it was going to be. That whole game was a special game for me.

"It was like a lesson you try to teach your kids about doing stuff the right way and working hard. We put our time in, all the blood and sweat."

The Browns went to the playoffs and lost to the archrival Steelers in Pittsburgh, 36-33.

"It was bittersweet for me," Wohlabaugh said. "When we sat in the locker room afterwards, I was basically saying goodbye to 53 guys. I knew it was my last game for the Browns."

Wohlabaugh was released two months later for salary cap reasons. He signed the next day with the St. Louis Rams.

TIM COUCH

The "Hail Mary pass" has been in football's lexicon only since 1975. Roger Staubach, the Hall of Fame quarterback of the Dallas Cowboys, coined the term to describe a last-second desperation pass that pulled out a miraculous victory.

The play is extremely rare. Circumstances have to be just right, and the chances of pulling it off are infinitesimal. A quarterback is lucky to experience it once in a lifetime.

Tim Couch has done it twice.

The Browns made Couch the NFL's No. 1 draft choice when they were resurrected as an expansion franchise in 1999.

Couch set numerous passing records in three years at University of Kentucky, but never won a game in college on a Hail Mary pass. He never did it as Kentucky's "Mr. Football" at Leslie County High School in tiny Hyden, Kentucky, either.

But in his rookie NFL season of 1999, the opportunity arose and Couch pulled it off.

The Browns were heading for their eighth consecutive loss to start their expansion season. Down by two points to New Orleans, Couch had time for one play from the Browns' 44-yard line.

"It was almost a hopeless situation," he recalled years later.

Couch took the snap in shotgun formation, circled to his right to gain a head of steam and launched the ball to the rafters of the Louisiana Superdome. As it floated down, the ball was tipped by a Saints defender into the hands of Kevin Johnson, who snatched it and got both feet down inside the right corner of the end zone.

The jubilant Browns raced from their sideline and buried Couch and Johnson beneath a pile of humanity and shoulder pads.

"I couldn't breathe on the bottom of the pile," Johnson said.

The play took the wind out of Saints coach Mike Ditka, too. He lay face down on the Superdome floor as the Browns pranced off with a 21-16 victory.

"That was probably the best part of all," Couch said. "It's a memory I'll never forget."

Three years later, Couch had a similar memory to file.

By the 2002 season, the Browns had made a coaching change and were on their way up. They pulled into Jacksonville with a 6-6 record, good enough to be in the thick of their division race.

The Jaguars were ahead, 17-14, and had the ball at the Browns' 10-yard line after a Couch interception with 1:25 to play. Three handoffs took the ball to the four. Jaguars coach Tom Coughlin then made a controversial decision he would regret.

Rather than try one more run to put the game away, Coughlin chose to kick a field goal and pad the Jacksonville lead to 20-14 with 50 seconds left. Commanding? Yes. But not insurmountable.

A shallow Jacksonville kickoff gave the Browns the ball at their 47. Two plays took the ball to the 50. The clock could not be stopped. The Browns appeared confused as they lined up with the clock ticking past 13 seconds.

Two receivers lined up on the left side and two on the right. Accepting the snap in the shotgun formation, Couch ducked from pressure and moved to his left, looking for Johnson, his accomplice in the 1999 game. Couch stepped up to gain momentum, looked again to his left and then threw the ball to the right corner of the end zone for Quincy Morgan.

Morgan, a big, physical receiver, jostled with Jacksonville cornerback Fernando Bryant and then pushed off with his left arm while he pulled in the ball with his right hand. When Morgan hit the ground, it appeared the ball squirted free, but the official on the spot signaled touchdown after a few agonizing seconds.

The play survived an instant replay review, and the Browns sweated out an extra point by Phil Dawson and won the game, 21-20.

Afterwards, Jacksonville linebacker Akin Ayodele said, "I've never been in a game like this." Most players never have.

But for Couch and his teammates, it was old hat. Two Hail Mary wins in four years.

CHRIS SPIELMAN

The Browns were skeptical when Massillon High School and Ohio State football legend Chris Spielman asked to finish his NFL career in Cleveland in the expansion season of 1999.

"That could be a nightmare for all of us," Dwight Clark, the general manager, told him.

Clark and the Browns feared that if Spielman, 34, was not good enough to play—or was not fully recovered from vertebrae fushion surgery in 1997—his popularity would make it impossible for the Browns to cut him.

"Trust me. I'll do the right thing," Spielman promised Clark.

In the months leading up to the Browns' first training camp, the fledgling franchise was energized by Spielman's intensity in the weight room.

But Spielman had not collided with a player or made a tackle in 21 months since suffering a broken neck in a 1997 game with the Buffalo Bills. Nobody knew if his neck could withstand the trauma of a violent NFL collision, or if Spielman could overcome the psychological barrier of exposing the neck to another injury.

The first test came in the first week of training camp. In a team drill, Spielman met Tarek Saleh, a 240-pound fullback, head on. Spielman took the brunt of the collision and lay on the ground for several moments as a hush descended on the practice fields. He left for the trainer's room on his own power.

A half-hour after practice ended, Spielman appeared outside the press room. In full uniform, he walked pensively onto the deserted fields holding his helmet in his left hand.

It took him about five minutes to reach the far end of the field. There, he buckled on his helmet and banged into a blocking sled with his right shoulder pad. And then his left. After doing this for a few minutes, he turned around and walked back, just as slowly.

Spielman suited up and played sparingly in the first three preseason games. In the third one, the first in new Cleveland Browns Stadium, Spielman suffered another collision.

He turned to defend a screen pass and ran into Chicago Bears center Casey Wiegmann. Spielman got hit from the blind side. He lay on the grass, not feeling anything for 12 seconds, before being helped off the field and taken to the Cleveland Clinic.

The next morning, Spielman walked into coach Chris Palmer's office and told him he intended to continue playing. Twelve hours later, he changed his mind. Palmer was relieved.

He retired two days later. The record book will show that Spielman never played a game for the Browns. But he made more of an impact that first training camp than many players who lasted the whole first season.

SPERGON WYNN

When injuries decimated the Browns' quarterback position in the 2000 season, a strapping, big-armed passer named Spergon Wynn got a taste of the limelight.

Wynn, 6'3" and 226 pounds, began his college career at Minnesota and then transferred to Southwest Texas State. In his senior year, he completed only 49.8 percent of passes, but impressed some scouts with his rocket arm.

The Browns drafted Wynn in the sixth round. With his limited background, the Browns envisioned developing Wynn over time as a backup quarterback. They never expected him to be thrust into action as a rookie.

But after Tim Couch broke a thumb in practice in the middle of the season, Wynn graduated to the No. 2 job behind journeyman Doug Pederson. Pederson was not effective, and fans clamored to see Wynn's big arm in a game.

So did Dwight Clark, the general manager.

At Clark's urging, coach Chris Palmer decided to give Wynn some playing time in the ninth game against Cincinnati. Palmer planned to insert Wynn on the Browns' third possession. Problem was, the Browns inherited the ball at their two-yard line, and Palmer did not deviate from his plan.

Wynn got out of the series alive and played five more possessions, proving what Palmer already knew—that he was not ready to play in an NFL game.

During this period, Wynn was a guest on Palmer's weekly television show. Sitting next to the coach during a commercial break, Wynn was so nervous that sweat squirted from his face like a lawn sprinkler.

By the time Wynn's guest segment was over, his shirt was drenched in perspiration.

At practice later in the week, Palmer said to an observer of the scene, "You see what I'm dealing with now?"

Five weeks later, Palmer had no recourse but to start Wynn after Pederson injured a finger on his throwing hand. Wynn's unfortunate start came in Jacksonville.

The Jaguars ravaged him for five sacks and injured his knee. Wynn limped off at halftime and continued to limp in the second half. Palmer kept him in almost the entire game.

Wynn completed five of 16 passes for 17 yards as the Browns suffered their worst defeat ever, 48-0. They had 53 yards total offense and two first downs, one as a result of a Jaguars penalty.

Wynn never threw another pass for the Browns. He was traded to Minnesota the following year.

Ben Gay

The Browns didn't know what to make of Ben Gay when they introduced the running back with the intriguing background to the media on the first day of their 2001 training camp.

"We're calling him Benjamin Gay," general manager Dwight Clark said. "He's such a mystery. He'll be very interesting to watch."

Gay was 21 when he arrived. He had virtually no football experience beyond his high school years in Houston. There he was nicknamed "Legend" and compared to Bo Jackson.

Butch Davis recruited Gay when he coached at the University of Miami. He reputedly had a 40 time of 4.38 seconds. For a back standing 6'1" and weighing 217 pounds, that speed opened eyes.

Gay had not played organized football in two years. He was kicked off the Baylor University team after one semester, and then played nine games for Garden City Community College in Kansas.

Gay hired an agent and signed with Edmonton of the Canadian Football League. After a couple weeks in training camp, he left abruptly to witness the birth of his daughter in Houston. He never returned.

That's why Davis called Gay an "80-to-1 longshot" to make the team, even though the Browns were desperate for a running back.

Within days, Gay lived up to his nickname.

The team's first intrasquad scrimmage drew an audience of 2,900 to training camp in Berea. As the No. 1 offense sputtered, fans lost patience and chanted, "We want Ben." A loud ovation erupted when Gay, wearing No. 34, trotted onto the field.

On Gay's fourth carry, he blasted through the line and sprinted 58 yards before getting knocked out of bounds. The fans stood and roared.

Afterwards, reporters surrounded Gay. "It was a beautiful day," he said. "I thank the fans for coming out to see me."

Gay's mysterious past wasn't the only thing unusual about him.

He thanked reporters each time they interviewed him. Early in training camp, Gay was leveled to the ground by a linebacker. Gay jumped to his feet, and as the players dispersed to other locations, Gay shook the hands of each member of the defense.

Teammates became skeptical of his odd behavior. They derisively referred to him as "Legend."

At times, though, Gay looked like the best player on the field. The 80-to-1 long shot made the team and became a fan favorite.

Gay did not carry the ball from scrimmage until the ninth game in Baltimore. He rushed 18 times for 56 yards and one touchdown as the Browns upset the rival Baltimore Ravens, who were defending Super Bowl champions.

On the surface, things were turning around for Gay. He was filling a vital need on the team.

An industrious fan created a Ben Gay website, on which Gay's face was superimposed on national monuments such as the Statue of Liberty and Mount Rushmore, and in action shots of famous athletes like Michael Jordan soaring for a slam dunk.

But then sordid details of Gay's past life bubbled to the surface.

In an interview in *The Plain Dealer*, Gay disclosed that during a time he was out of football and working as a bouncer in a bar, he peddled drugs and fired a gun at people several times.

In the story, his coach at Garden City said, "Ben Gay could walk into the White House in a tuxedo and schmooze the president. But in the next instant, he'd turn into the biggest gutter rat, fink, slime-bucket you've ever known. He's full of charm and charisma, but he'd rather tell a lie when the truth would do just fine."

Behind the scenes, Gay was arriving late for team meetings and failing to report to weightlifting sessions. On the field, he was bungling assignments and fumbling. He became unpopular with teammates. Club officials distanced themselves from him after his drug revelations.

He carried the ball in four other games and finished third on the team with 172 yards rushing.

After the season, Davis said, "There won't be anybody in this league that has much more talent than him."

In their next draft, the Browns selected running back William Green with their top choice. Gay was released a week later.

"When we signed him, we knew there was a risk," Davis said. "We gave the guy the benefit of doubt that he would mature."

Gay was signed by the Indianapolis Colts shortly thereafter. They released him in training camp.

Celebrate the Heroes of Professional Football
in These Other 2004 Releases from Sports Publishing!

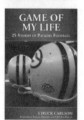

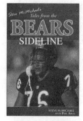